PRAISE FOR *OUR*

MW01614857

Our Names Do Not Appear is a vivid memoir of the heroine's quest for an understanding of the void left in her life by the infant death of a younger brother. Reaching across decades and spanning cultural distances between Cleveland and Jerusalem, Lev's quest leads to an intimate re-imagining of her own experience of family trauma. **A richly moving story of a woman's growth to insight and compassion.**

> Avivah Gottlieb Zornberg, author of *The Murmuring Deep: Reflections on the Biblical Unconscious*

Hineni, here I am, asserts Judy Lev in this aptly titled memoir, *Our Names Do Not Appear*. In a woven trilogy, a triple elegy, part fairy tale, part investigative journalism, the memoir moves from 1950s Ohio to end-of-century Jerusalem. **Lev's tender alchemy of forgiveness and love is a triumph of the spirit and the imagination.**

> Marcela Sulak, co-author of *Family Resemblance: An Anthology and Exploration of 8 Hybrid Literary Genres*

Held captive by a familial tragedy she cannot remember, Judy Lev liberates herself through constructing an astonishing narrative. Lev renders her younger brother's forgotten death in striking prose, engages the fictive imagination in the father's first-person narrative, and employs an analytic intellect in courageous personal essays. ***Our Names Do Not Appear* is a bold literary tour de force that transcends genre—a searing triumph of postmodernism!**

> Allen Hoffman, author of the Small Worlds series

How do you tell a complex family story of love, loss, secrecy, grief, revelation, and forgiveness? Judy Lev's answer is through a multiplicity of forms and genres. In this lyrical, imaginative hybrid memoir, she pieces together the story of her baby brother's brief life, a taboo subject in her family, through letters and documents, the fictionalized version of her father's experience of Joey's birth and death and the introspective story of Lev's quest to reach a deeper understanding of her parents and herself. **Our Names Do Not Appear is an engrossing, brilliantly written jewel of a book.**

Lisa Knopp, author of *The Nature of Home: A Lexicon and Essays*

Our Names Do Not Appear recounts the solving of a personal and deeply troubling family mystery story—part investigation, part imaginative tale. It unfolds as an engrossing, gorgeous, and intimate account of a woman's life-long passage from childhood innocence through haunting grief to a mature reckoning with self and family, leading us through Jewish tradition, culture, and history to a place of peace and enlightenment—for both the author and the reader. **Our Names Do Not Appear is a powerful and moving story, a book that matters.**

Philip Gerard, author of *Creative Nonfiction: Researching and Crafting Stories of Real Life*

OUR NAMES DO NOT APPEAR

A Memoir

By

Judy Lev

ISBN: 978-1-957712-07-9 (paperback)

ISBN: 978-1-957712-08-6 (ebook)

Publisher: Lioness Books

LIBRARY OF CONGRESS Cataloguing-in-Publication Data

Our Names Do Not Appear / Judy Lev

1. Memoir   2. Grief   3. Women's Literature

We are, I am, you are
by cowardice or courage
the one who find our way
back to this scene
carrying a knife, a camera
a book of myths
in which
our names do not appear.

Adrienne Rich, "Diving into the Wreck"

TABLE OF CONTENTS

This is a memoir that respects the realistic use of imagination to deal with grief.

Some names have been changed to protect the privacy of loved ones.

Part One: Give Sorrow Words

Give sorrow words; the grief that does not speak
Whispers the o'er-fraught heart, and bids it break.

William Shakespeare, *Macbeth*, Act IV, Scene 3

Chapter One: Earthquake

Baby Joseph was dying in the next room. For three days he had suffered from diarrhea, his fever shooting up to 103.8. I stood at the kitchen sink, looking at Jerusalem while peeling carrots. One chicken, almost the size of Joseph, roasted in the oven. Another chicken sat in the soup pot waiting for its italian parsley. The pockets of my gray apron that Grandma had made for my mother and that my mother had handed down to me were filled with damp tissues.

Across the street Mr. Ben Eli was locking his corner grocery. The Bulgarian butcher next door to him had already gone home. In two hours the Sabbath would descend on Jerusalem the way a bride descends a high staircase to meet her beloved on her wedding day—slowly, each step drenched in ethereal light.

As usual, Elliott lounged on the living room couch reading the weekend *Jerusalem Post*. In our bedroom Joseph lay in the middle of the bed, limp and apathetic. His sister, Miriam, older by two years, kept watch. When Miriam ran screaming into the kitchen, from his roost Elliott ordered calm.

"But he's shaking," Miriam cried. "Come see."

I ran into the bedroom, wiping my hands on the apron. Joseph, naked, lay on his back on the bed. The clean cloth diaper that had covered him now lay on the floor.

"Did you take that off?" I screamed at Miriam.

She grabbed my apron and hid behind it. "No," she whispered. "He shook it off."

"What do you mean? What did you see?" I felt stupid relying on the description of a small child.

She told me she was sitting on Abba's side of the bed and suddenly saw Joseph's arms shake. She shook her arm to show me. "I told him to stop, but then his leg shook."

I felt Joseph's forehead. He was burning up. I picked up the diaper and threw it to Miriam. "Bring this. Come with me." We walked past Elliot, who was standing at the door to the bedroom, watching.

In the bathroom I put the baby on a towel on top of the washing machine. "Wet the diaper," I shouted at Miriam.

"I'll call the doctor," my husband said, sticking his head in. "Don't worry, everything will be okay."

Miriam threw me a wet diaper. I rubbed Joseph's body and prayed that his temperature would go down, away, to another house, not mine. My baby was on fire.

Elliot came back with the doctor's message: If it happens again, take him to the hospital. Bikur Cholim is on duty.

"It's Friday afternoon," I shouted.

"So what?" he said. "The doctor says it could be dangerous."

The damp diaper worked its magic. Slowly Joseph's temperature went down. I dressed him lightly and put him back in the middle of the bed. "Watch him," I told Miriam, who was following me.

In the kitchen I threw celery, carrots, salt, and pepper into the soup pot, filled it with water, and lit the flame. I spread the white tablecloth on our dining table and stacked the white plates, white napkins, kiddush cup, and silverware. I hoped Joseph would fall asleep until after dinner. Then he could sleep in his own bed until morning, when he would awake healthy.

"Come, Ema," Miriam screamed.

I ran to her. Elliot followed.

Joseph's arms and legs were shaking. His brown eyes rolled into his head, as if he had been snatched by a demon. I had never seen anything like it.

"Stop it," I screamed. "Stop shaking."

Elliot told me to calm down.

"How can I calm down? Why don't you do something?"

He ran into the bathroom and brought a damp washcloth. I started to cry, then shouted louder at Joseph. "Please, stop it, Joey. Stop shaking." Miriam hid behind me.

Elliot said we should go to the hospital and I should relax. How could I relax? My baby was dying. My third child. My smiley, happy, beautiful, innocent eight-month-old baby was dying.

Miriam whimpered, peeked from behind me, and said, "Joseph stopped."

I thought she meant he had stopped breathing. "No, don't die," I yelled.

My husband grabbed my arm. "Honey, get hold of yourself. It's okay. See? He's not shaking."

I ran into the kitchen to call a cab.

"We don't need a fucking cab," Elliot shouted. He held Joseph over his shoulder as he stormed into the kitchen. "I'll drive."

I wrapped the baby in a lightweight blanket. It was October, the evenings were cool. Fortunately, Michael was sleeping at a friend's house. The last thing I saw before leaving our apartment was the silver candlesticks on the marble counter, waiting to be lit.

We dropped Miriam off with the downstairs neighbors. "Of course she can stay here," said beloved Shoshana. "Miriam can help me set the table."

I sat in the back seat holding Joseph. The roads were empty. Candles flickered in apartment windows above the closed shops on Bethlehem Road, King David Street, and Jaffa Road, suggesting familial warmth. The news on the radio said something about King Hassan of Morocco meeting with Reagan in the White House. More peace proposals. I clutched Joseph to my chest. If I held him tightly, he couldn't shake. To repel the ensuing darkness, I sang, "This little light of mine, I'm gonna let it shine . . ."

"Faster," I yelled.

"Be quiet and let me drive," Elliott shouted.

Downtown was deserted. We made it to Bikur Cholim in eight minutes, which still felt too long. Elliot pulled into the driveway opposite the emergency room. Clutching

Joseph to my chest, I ran inside the old building. "Where's a doctor? Where's a doctor?"

The security guard, an old man sitting at the door, immersed in Psalms, pointed a wrinkled finger to the left, barely lifting his head.

A young nurse told me to be quiet. "This is a hospital. Respect the Sabbath."

The emergency room smelled sour. All the metal and plastic surfaces made me want to roar. Even the sheets looked hard.

A white-coated man with black hair and glasses approached. He asked what the problem was, lifting Joseph from my arms. As soon as he placed the baby on the examination table, the trembling began.

"Look. He's shaking. See his arms. Look at his eyes. It's the third time since three thirty." I spoke as if the doctor were deaf and dumb.

"Okay, okay," he said. "He's having a convulsion." He turned to the young nurse. "Time it, Rivka."

Elliot walked into the ER and stood behind me. He placed his hand on my left shoulder. How long had it been since that had happened? Our baby quivered and shook like the shelves, paintings, and books in our living room had rumbled six years earlier during an earthquake. That was the day I realized anyone could die without warning.

"It's a convulsion," I told Elliot.

"Yes," he said. "Convulsion."

Saying and hearing the word offered hope and despair. I told the doctor that my son had never had a convulsion before. I wanted to sound competent and calm. I wanted the staff to know that Joseph was the result of a healthy pregnancy, a normal birth at the end of nine months—a baby who loved throwing himself onto pillows, crawling, climbing, and pulling himself into a standing position on the bookshelves. I wanted the staff to know that his mother was neither negligent nor hysterical. This baby was a smiler, a *lover-oppolus*, a Curious George. This third child of mine was a one hundred percent healthy baby.

"Let's go home," I said to Elliot. "I want to light candles. I want you to chant kiddush and hold Joseph on your lap. I don't like hospitals."

Elliot's kiddush was the pride of our family. He sang in a deep, rich voice, taking his time, enunciating each word, always in tune, looking thoroughly Israeli in his white shirt open at the neck to reveal a chest of hair the color of *hamra*, the rich, warm earth of the Sharon plain, brown with a mischievous tint of red. That was the earth he loved to till and tread when he had first come to Israel from Toronto as a sixteen-year-old in 1959, when he took off his Canadian boots and donned Israeli sandals for an eight-month visit. In late June of 1967, after the war, Elliot came back to Israel and mastered Hebrew. He completed his transformation from Canadian to Israeli by working on a new kibbutz on the Golan Heights, where he morphed into the handsome, iconic kibbutznik—Paul Newman with a moustache. That was the romantic facade, the image, the mask I fell for when we first met in Jerusalem in 1969, his kibbutz days already history.

Elliot, who insisted on being called Eli outside the house, was my key to Israeli life, lore, and geography, or so I told myself. We traveled the country in our VW bug, slept in tents, celebrated Passover on the shores of Sinai, adoring Israel as if the land were a new mother, a loving mother for both of us, her arms open wide, beckoning her lost children home.

"One hundred and twenty seconds," said Rivka.

"Take him upstairs," the doctor told Elliot. Then, turning to Rivka, he said, "I want a full blood and urine workup."

He pointed us to the elevator. "Second floor. Turn right." He handed Joseph to my husband.

In the hallway outside the children's ward, a student nurse took the baby and showed us to a green Formica bench. I wanted to protest but didn't. An eerie darkness and quiet reigned in the hallway, because of either the Sabbath or financial cuts. I wanted Elliot to place his palm on my head like he had on our first date, when we saw *Bonnie and Clyde*. That was the first sign that I would marry him. I wanted him to tell me everything would be all right, but after I sat down on the bench, he went downstairs for a smoke.

After twenty minutes another nurse brought me my Joseph. He was wearing green starched pajamas three sizes too big. On the chest pocket that covered his torso were the words "Bikur Cholim," printed in black Hebrew and English letters.

"Press hard on the cotton swab on the neck," said the nurse. She sounded like she was talking about a lamb, not my son. I lifted the cotton and saw a bloody hole in Joseph's neck. He lay loose in my arms, squishy like cookie dough, too tired to cry. I drew him to my heart and held him tightly, hating Israeli hospitals and hating Elliot for leaving me alone.

A woman doctor approached. Before she opened her mouth, her eyes told me she was determined to help. "We have to hospitalize him," she said, in a calm, understanding tone, "to figure out why he's convulsing . . . He's a beautiful baby, your Joseph." I wanted to throw my arms around this woman, put my head on her chest, and cry.

In the ward Joseph settled onto a low mattress in a bed with high iron slats—an inmate, imprisoned in a child's cell. He stared at the harsh fluorescent light on the ceiling high above. I pulled up a wobbly iron chair and watched him breathe. He *was* a beautiful little boy—brown eyes that shone easily, straight brown hair that covered his forehead with wispy Vs and Ws, lips born to smile and showing three teeth. We had named him after my grandfather.

All I knew about Joseph Steinberg was that he had had red hair and a fierce temper that invoked fear in his five children and that he settled in Fort Dodge, Iowa, in the late 1890s, having immigrated to the US from Moldova, entering the new continent at International Falls, Minnesota. As I thought about Joseph's namesake, I felt ashamed of how little I knew about him and also his son, my father.

Staring at Joseph, I remembered the other reason we chose the name. Joseph was the baby brother who had died when I was a little girl. As my thoughts traveled from Iowa to Cleveland, my Jerusalem Joseph started to tremble and shake.

"Convulsion, convulsion," I yelled, running toward the nurses' station. When I returned, Joseph's face was magenta, purple, and turning darker shades of blue. Two nurses entered the room.

"Oxygen," commanded one to the other. "Put his head in the center. I want an IV ready. Get the child neurologist down here. Put a rush on those tests."

I had never seen anything like it, a baby's face turning to the dark side of the rainbow. The end of day at sunset. I couldn't bear watching, so I ran to the ladies' room opposite the ward, opened the door, and sat on a cold toilet seat. I was losing my Joseph. This was how it happened: a Friday night, lights shining in every Jerusalem home, and my little light fades.

It feels good to be alone in a small space. It feels good to be numb, alone, and grave. My breathing stops when I imagine Joseph dead. I think of my mother. I want to tell her, *Now I know you. Now I'm like you.* It happens so quickly. You're standing at the kitchen sink peeling a carrot while your son begins to die in the next room. Time is taut. You try to get help, but there is no help, no savior, no refuge.

When I begin to breathe again, I, a mother who has lost her baby, walk calmly into the ward as though in a trance. An oxygen mask hangs on the edge of Joseph's bed.

"Let's go," I say to Elliot, who is standing next to Joseph's bed, smelling like a cheap cigarette.

"What do you mean let's go?" His eyes say I am crazy.

"He's dead," I say. "I want to leave. I want to go home."

A nurse fidgeting nearby comes over to me and, rather than yell, says in a loud whisper that I am insane. "You think it's so easy to die?" She reminds me of my father, who used to make me feel stupid. "Your son is just fine. *You* go home."

I kneel to the level of Joseph's mattress. He isn't purple or blue. His lips are poised in a smile, his eyes shut. Air exits his nose. Joseph lives. Still.

Standing up while holding the bars of his cot, I look around at the other babies in the ward, all breathing, sleeping, or drinking. And I wonder why. Why did I kill my baby?

Chapter Two: Tornado

Joey died when I was three or four. Maybe five.

Nobody took me to his grave.

For a long time I thought he was just gone and would come back.

Once, in a box of family photos in a cabinet on the upstairs landing, I saw an oval photo of a baby, hair still wet from the birth canal. Two eyes stared at me, pleading. Was this sprite my baby brother?

* * *

Rabbi Green comes to the house. He sits on the striped living room couch with its dull hues of yellow, chartreuse, and brown, its fabric smooth as Jell-O. The couch is perfect for jumping, but Elizabeth and I are not allowed to jump in the house. We stand still in front of the rabbi, like the stiff ceramic dog on the breakfront shelf. The rabbi's name is Green, but he wears black pants and a white shirt. I wonder what he does when he is not talking for God.

Above him hangs a painting of an Iowa farm. A tornado rushes from the right side of the gold picture frame. Soon the red barn, white silo, gray wooden farmhouse, and fields of swaying green corn will fly away. The dark, wild sky will devour all. No person stirs; Iowa's empty.

When I dare look straight into Rabbi Green's face, Iowa corn grows from his bare head.

"Come closer, girls," he says. "I have something sad to tell you."

He lowers sadness over his face like a window shade. With his right hand he holds my left and with his left he holds Elizabeth's right. His hand is smooth, like warm butter.

This is the first time the rabbi has come to our house, the first time anyone has said, "I have something sad to tell you."

Ours is the upstairs floor of a two-family house: 2849 Ludlow Road, Cleveland, Ohio, one block away from Shaker Heights. My father says Shaker Heights is the

Valley of God's Pleasure. Our living room is still, the three of us small compared to the height of the room. Green stucco walls soar and curve toward each other at the top, tall as six fathers. It's like a castle. From the ceiling hangs a gold chandelier with five branches. I fear floating to the ceiling and being sucked through a secret hole, released into space, my thumb in my mouth. Who will save me?

Song saves me. On Sunday afternoons Elizabeth and I climb the narrow twisting staircase to the upstairs landing. We sit there overlooking the living room and cover our heads with brown blankets as we sing:

> "Aba daba daba daba daba daba dab,"
> Said the chimpie to the monk.
> "Baba daba daba daba daba dab,"
> Said the monkey to the chimp.

We like to sing, but not today. With the rabbi holding our shy hands we stand in silence.

"I have something very sad to tell you," he says, and because this is the second time and he says *very*, I believe he is telling the truth.

Outside, snow falls like macaroni. It buries the front lawn, the elm, the fire hydrant and sidewalk. Frozen noodles hang on bare branches. Everything is iced in place and time, even the rabbi's voice when he says the words: "Your baby brother Joey died."

I giggle, because I don't know how else to be.

Know-it-all Elizabeth pokes me with her left elbow. "Shhhh," she shushes.

The rabbi is holding our little hands. Our mother is standing at the kitchen sink. Our father reads Sunday's *Cleveland Plain Dealer* in his room, smoking a Camel.

The rabbi's eyes peer from behind thick circles of glass. Gold wires hold the eyeglasses in place. Gold threads separate some of the ugly brown and chartreuse stripes on the living room couch. The rabbi's pale face is blotched with red spots, like my father's. Maybe his parents came from Moldova, too. The rabbi's lips are thick and soft, like mine. Does he suck his thumb? How does God pay him? The rabbi's face looks as if the tornado has hit the Iowa barn, but he does not run away.

"Now repeat after me," he says. "The Lord is my shepherd . . ."

Elizabeth and I repeat. Shepherds wear striped coats of many colors. Does the Lord wear a coat? The rabbi's coat is black. He gave it to my father to hang up.

"I shall not want . . ."

My stomach grumbles. It's Sunday and I want warm french toast with canadian bacon, smothered in Aunt Jemima's Original Syrup. Her bosom on the front of the bottle is big as a beach ball and soft as a cloud. I want my mother's chocolate chip cookies for dessert. I want to sit at the table with everyone—Elizabeth, my mother, father, Joey, even Grandma, who lives with us now.

"He leadeth me beside the still waters . . ."

Downtown, near my father's creamery full of butter and eggs, flow the stinky still waters of the Cuyahoga River.

"Though I walk through the valley of the shadow of death . . ."

Is the Valley of God's Pleasure near the valley of the shadow of death? Death may be catching.

". . . and I shall dwell in the House of the Lord forever."

Could 2849 be the House of the Lord? Is today part of forever?

We repeat the words after the rabbi as if they are true. I know I am promising something or going somewhere, but I have no idea what or where.

Right after *forever*, my father walks into the living room, smelling like a Camel, carrying the rabbi's black coat, and swinging the *Cleveland Plain Dealer*. He has rolled it into a bat. I take my hands back to myself, burst out crying, and run from the rabbi to the dining room, around the oval table and its six heavy chairs, into the kitchen.

Like a still life, my mother stands at the sink. I grab the left side of her gray apron, bawling, wailing, sniffling, choking with sobs. My nose runs; tears blur my eyes. Fluids drown me from inside and out.

My mother holds herself upright at the stainless steel sink, facing the window, feet firm on the gray linoleum floor. She could be scrubbing a pot, peeling a potato, or staring. Maybe she's watching the water drip from the faucet or looking at the macaroni snow fall from the sky onto the garage's black roof. The snow falls slowly, forever, outside time. Does she know Joey died?

Grandma sewed the gray apron that falls from my mother's shoulders and covers her hips. Forsythia buds flutter over the apron like small birds seeking a home. Damp Kleenex tissues live in the deep pockets on the sides and front. I hide my wet face in her gray-aproned body.

Elizabeth stands on the other side. When did she get here? Is she crying? Is our mother? I hear only my sobs. Mother says nothing. She continues to stand upright at the sink, leaning slightly against the counter. What else can support?

My father stomps into the kitchen, waving his arms, hitting invisible baseballs with the *Cleveland Plain Dealer*.

I clutch the strings of the apron for life.

"Now will you stop crying, Judy?" he shouts. "Enough already. You're outta line."

He comes closer and stands next to me. I bury my face in the pockets of my mother's apron. If I were a baby kangaroo, I would crawl inside. The refrigerator cackles and hums, hums and cackles.

"Don't upset your mother," he yells. "Leave her alone," he shouts. "Be quiet!"

His shouts strike my upper back. They rip the skin. My breathing backs up, stutters, and stalls.

My mother stands still at the kitchen sink, arms stiff as icicles.

My father stands above me, strange as a camel in Iowa. I fear he may pitch a deathblow with his paper bat. For safety I sink into the gray linoleum floor. It clamps over me like iron. Here I shall dwell, close to forever.

Chapter Three: Past Present

During the weeks after Joseph's hospitalization, he returned to being the playful baby he had been before his convulsions, as if he had never turned magenta and blue, slept in an oxygen tent, or received saline solution in his tiny veins, as if he had never been punctured by smiling as well as nasty nurses in every finger and vein, never handled by every pediatric neurologist on staff at Bikur Cholim, never belted down on a table so a CAT scan could check him for damage. His prognosis was good, provided the convulsions didn't return.

I, however, cried easily and often—in the shower, in bed, while reading Michael and Miriam "Zlateh the Goat." All day, every day, I thought about Joey, my baby brother who had died . . . or not, for I had no proof, only a memory of the day Rabbi Green sat on the couch. Maybe I had made up the scene of the rabbi holding our hands. Maybe I had been jumping on the couch and my father had yelled at me and I ran into the kitchen and clung to my mother's apron and she would not comfort me because she agreed with my father that little girls should not jump on the sofa. True, I never saw Joey after the rabbi's visit; I didn't know for sure if I had *ever* seen Joey. If there was no grave, perhaps he still lived . . . in Elyria, Wooster, or Akron. Or if there was no grave, perhaps he was never born and I wanted a baby brother so much that my imagination gave birth to Joey.

During the months after Joseph's hospitalization, I craved facts: dates, locations, names, diagnoses, and cause of death. My own Joseph's medical report from Bikur Cholim, signed by Dr. Shalev, a pediatric neurologist, in November 1982, declared his convulsions had stemmed from hyponatremia, a condition of low sodium due to diarrhea. This report and these facts comforted me. I wanted truthful, real documents about my baby brother Joey, texts infallible and staunch as Mount Zion.

Once, several months after Joseph's recovery, in a late-night telephone conversation with my mother, I mentioned as if in passing that I had been thinking about Joey. After a brief silence my mother said, "Joey? You mean . . . your baby brother?"

I had never mentioned him to her before, afraid the name itself might upset her. Was the subject still taboo? I didn't want her to know I was so obsessed that I was ignoring my own sons and daughter because of the disappearance of her third child and first son. I certainly did not tell her of family dinners when Miriam would stare at me through the vegetable soup, her four-year-old eyes mapping my face, reading my sadness and thoughts, and how at the end of the meal she would whisper, her voice scared, "Ema. Ema, come back."

I did not tell my mother that my husband called me Little Miss Lost-in-the-Past. Those were the good days. On the bad days Elliot yelled at me to shape up, set boundaries, take control. He threw potholders and damp bath towels onto my desk when, after the children went to sleep, I tried to recreate the scene of the rabbi sitting on the couch, thinking one written scene might trigger another and eventually give me back my past. My husband's rhetorical refrain hummed in my ears: "Why does the house always have to look like a shithole?"

"Joey?" my mother repeated, surprised, as if I had mentioned Harry Truman.

Before I could reply, she asked about the current winter in Jerusalem. "Florida is so beautiful this time of year," she said. "I don't know why it took us so long to leave Cleveland. Leaving is so hard, but last winter made it easier."

The taboo was firmly in place. As hard as it was to broach the subject of Joey with my mother, talking with my father was not even an option. We never spoke about anything. Phone conversations with him began with his asking, "Everything under control over there?" and ended two seconds later after my answering in the affirmative, with, "Well, that's just ginger peachy. Now here's your mom." Had I asked him about Joey, he probably would have yelled at me for wasting time—"Why don't you start earning some money over there?"—and then, as always, would have handed the phone to my mother.

Once, when I was in my midtwenties, I had asked Elizabeth about Joey. We were standing at another kitchen sink, this one in her New York apartment on the Upper West Side, cleaning green beans. She told me that she thought Joey had been retarded or had Down's syndrome or something like that. She wasn't sure which. She said nobody ever spoke to her about Joey, but she didn't seem to care as much as I did.

"After six years in therapy," she said, rinsing a batch of beans, "I overcame my guilt for killing him."

The knife in my hand fell into the sink. I braced myself against the counter and with great effort asked, "You killed him?"

"No, no," she said, grabbing my knife to scrape the tips of the beans into the garbage. "I only *fantasized* killing him. I have no idea what happened to him."

Grandma, the best source of information, had been dead for sixteen years.

I was on my own. The only person who could possibly provide information and resurrect that winter afternoon was the messenger himself, Rabbi Green. I had had an amicable relationship with him when I attended Sunday school at his Temple Emanu El. He had blessed me by placing his hands on my head at consecration, when I was six and received my own Torah scroll (a hand-me-down from Elizabeth), and again when I was fifteen, at confirmation, which marked the end of Sunday school. Years later, after the Six-Day War, when he and his wife had visited Jerusalem, I went to see them at the Moriah Hotel. We chatted. He took an interest in my Hebrew studies, proud and a little surprised that a former congregant was drawn to decipher the holy tongue and live down the block from the House of the Lord.

One morning in March of 1983, when all the children were out of the house and I had three glorious hours to myself, I sat down at my desk and wrote what would become the first of many letters.

Dear Rabbi Green,

This letter may come as a shock after so many years, but you are the only person in the world who can help me. A little background to bring you up to date. As I told you when we last met in the fall of '67, I came to Jerusalem for a year to learn Hebrew. While I was studying Hebrew, I realized there was another language I had to learn, this one harder. The sacred center turned inward, so I stayed. And stayed. Sometimes I think I stay in Jerusalem to figure out why I am staying—certainly, at least, to figure out who I am.

I am married to an immigrant who loves Israel as much as I do. We have three healthy children. Last October when Joseph, my youngest, was eight months old, he was hospitalized due to recurring convulsions. He suffered from hyponatremia, survived the ordeal beautifully, and returned to his active self. From the first Friday night in the hospital, I feared Joseph was dead. Ever since, I have been a nervous wreck. I can't believe he didn't die, as if he, the third child, a son, was scripted to disappear, like my brother Joey did. I look at him climbing on Miriam and

Michael, scaling the bookshelves in the living room, and I can't figure out what he's doing here.

On that first night when he turned purple and they put him in an oxygen tent, I thought of my mother and her Joey and the day—a Sunday, right?—you came over to the house on Ludlow to tell Elizabeth and me our baby brother died. All I remember from that period (1948? 1951?) is your coming to our house at 2849 Ludlow Road during a snowstorm. You sat on the couch and stood us in front of you. You held our hands. Then you told us Joey died and asked us to repeat after you the twenty-third psalm.

I have only one sentence for an event that proved a seminal crossroads in my life. That sentence is "The rabbi came to the house to tell us Joey died." I've embellished that sentence with sounds, sensations, colors as much as I can to resurrect that visit, that hour. Or was it five minutes? I want to go back to that couch and replay the scene, animate the stillness, vivify the sounds, relive the smells. I have no idea how. There is an emptiness inside me I want to fill with truth.

I need facts, Rabbi.

Sometimes at night, behind a book or in the solace of a shower, I cry. These tears are for Joey. But who was Joey? When did he die? From what? Why didn't anyone ever mention his name? Where is he buried? Why the secrets?

Any information you can pull up from the cistern of your memory will be greatly appreciated.

I tried to talk to my mother about Joey, but it is still taboo. I have never spoken with my father about anything. You know how stubborn he can be. Do you remember sitting next to him at the shiva for my grandmother? He asked you why the younger generation was so against the war in Vietnam. I was a student at the University of Michigan at that time. You said, "Why don't you ask your daughter? She's sitting right next to you." You witnessed. He couldn't even look at me, let alone talk.

Elizabeth once told me Joey was mentally retarded or suffered from Down's syndrome. She doesn't know anything else. When you were in Jerusalem in October

1967, I was studying Hebrew. I wanted to explore the past of the Jewish people. Now, as I spend most of my time mothering three children, the past that beckons is my own. I need facts, Rabbi. Can you help?

I must close now and pick up Joseph. Hoping you and your family are well and sending you warmest regards,

Judy

I read the letter and felt guilty for the length. Rabbi Green was a busy man, but I knew if I took the time to cut and rewrite, I would never send it. I folded it into thirds and stuffed it into an airmail envelope, licked an airmail stamp, addressed the envelope by hand, and put it in my purse. I put on my coat, for March had surprised us with cold days, even though Passover was only three weeks away. I left the apartment, locked the door behind me, and, on the way to pick up Joseph, dropped the letter into the mailbox on Bethlehem Road. As I continued to walk toward the house where Joseph was in a playgroup with two other one-year-olds, I felt something small and delicate lift from deep inside, as if some inner clamp had loosened.

Chapter Four: Molech

While waiting for the rabbi's reply, I developed an interest in Canaanite cults. One night, when Elliot watched TV in the room for the living and my children slept, I lay in bed engrossed in Molech stories. Molech was the pagan god to whom, two thousand seven hundred years earlier, Canaanites and some rebellious Israelites offered child sacrifices. In the Valley of Hinnom below Mount Zion, parents offered their live children to find favor with the ruling god. I had first encountered Molech during my visit to Mount Zion in 1966, when I was a twenty-one-year-old innocent and impressionable tourist.

* * *

It is late morning, August 3, 1966, and I am walking alone through the barren Valley of Hinnom. Sixteenth-century stone walls in the Jordanian Old City of Jerusalem act as a frontier before me. A nineteenth-century windmill behind me, in Israel's Yemin Moshe neighborhood, stands paralyzed. The sun beats the beige and gray rocks into submission on the valley floor. Nobody told me to wear a hat or bring water. My lips are cracked and sweat drips from my neck onto my cotton sleeveless shirt. I cross the asphalt road that winds through the valley, my dusty sandals burning with heat.

I am on my way to King David's Tomb because I have accepted Cantor Bushman's invitation. A part-time opera singer, Bushman stood on the pulpit at Temple Emanu El shoulder to shoulder with Rabbi Green. "Come ye," he sang, "and let us go up to the mountain of the Lord." I was eleven, curled into a cocoon in the last row of the sanctuary, bored. Going up a mountain appealed to a girl in a midwestern city where one of the main attractions was the Flats. Here I was, ten years later, climbing the mountain of the Lord. "And He will teach us of His ways, and we will walk in His paths," Bushman's voice echoes from my childhood, "for out of Zion shall go forth the law and the word of the Lord from Jerusalem."

I'm thirsty for water and hungry for the word, because I'm twenty-one and don't know who I am.

My only companion, Zev Vilnay's *The Guide to Israel*, ninth edition, says King David's Tomb is "one of the most revered of the Holy Places in the State of Israel." Only a description such as this will keep me walking through the Valley of Hinnom, otherwise known as Gehenna, or Hell. This dry ravine, which Vilnay claims is the site of the Molech sacrifices, feels like the valley of the shadow of death. There is no shade. The Sultan's Pool, a limestone basin on my left, has been cracked and dry for centuries. From every thorn and thistle, the landscape whispers, *Death*. As the sun pounds its evil fire onto me, I push forward to leave this diabolical ground. Surely the Ministry of Tourism will have placed a drinking fountain on top of Mount Zion.

* * *

In the book on my lap I fingered through several renditions of Molech. He had the head of a bull and the body of a man in the largest drawing. According to the explanation underneath, small children were placed as sacrificial offerings in Molech's outstretched hands and lowered into the bottom half of his body, where a fire blazed. The watching crowds of parents and believers gathered around Molech's molten image, screaming and drumming as the children burned. In another drawing Molech's hands, laden with small children, were in the process of being raised to his mouth, where the fire raged. My favorite rendition was Molech as a human god, with a crown of thorns and a deep hole where his penis wasn't.

In that deep hole burned the fire. Parents threw their children into that hole, hoping their supplications and gifts would cause Molech to favor them.

* * *

Searching for a stone stairway, I hear murmuring. No, that muffled eerie sound is too soft to be called murmuring. It is more like an echo of a sound, seeping up through the parched earth from the *tehom*, that vast abyss that existed before God created worlds and words. Or maybe it's not coming from the abyss, maybe it's the still cries of children sacrificed thousands of years ago, cries soaked into the ground I walk on. I imagine mothers and fathers throwing their sons and daughters into the Molech cauldrons, musicians beating on drums. *Dum tak tak dum tak*. An orgy of blood, screams, and drumming. The landscape has absorbed it all—rivers of blood, *dum tak tak dum tak*, screams of dying babies, *dum tak tak dum tak*, the wails of ambivalent mothers, *dum tak tak dum tak*, echoes of the sacrifices.

Could this be the word that goes out from Jerusalem?

Eventually I find the stone stairway leading up to Mount Zion. With every step I want to believe I am climbing the mountain of the Lord, but after ten minutes, when I reach the top, I feel deceived by this hoax of a beginner's ski slope. At least mature pines provide a little longed-for shade. Hyssop and rosemary fill my dry nose with sweet scents. At least there is, finally, a sign. The

Ministry of Tourism is pointing me in the direction of King David's Tomb. It is now the crypt of a large crusader church dedicated to Saint Mary. Upstairs, in the stone dining room, Jesus and his disciples ate their last supper, but who has the strength to climb to the top floor in the middle of a dry August day?

Following signs, I descend three stone steps into a cool dark cave. Small holes in the walls of the cave hold short white candles. Their flicker creates spooky shadows. Six old women, wearing shapeless flowered dresses that make them look like large bears, pink and orange kerchiefs draped over their heads, and gold earrings dangling from their ears, are standing together in the shadows. They hold prayer books in their hands. They face King David's Tomb. When I enter they stop their prayers and look at me, size me up as a lost blond American tourist, and return to their business, not even offering me a cup of the grapefruit juice I see tucked in their satchels.

King David's Tomb is a large marble sepulcher covered with a purple coverlet decorated with gold-embroidered words I can't read. From the size of the tomb, David grew to become a Goliath. The ancient Hebrew king is less real to me than Johnny Appleseed, so despite Vilnay's explanations and the coolness of the cave, I leave quickly.

* * *

Suddenly Elliot's face hovered over my book. "Can't you throw out old food?"

This was often his way of getting my attention.

"Why is something blue growing at the back of the fridge?"

At that moment, lost as I was on Mount Zion in August 1966, I had an answer neither worthy of a sentence nor worthy of his possible caring about the state of the fridge. He gave me one of his dirty looks and flung the Yiddish word *nahrishkeit* over my head, as in, "What is that *nahrishkeit* you're reading?"

I looked at his angry eyes and his moustache, the lips I often loved to kiss, and thought about the gun in the top drawer of his night table. He insisted on keeping a gun in the house so he could defend his family in case of a terror attack. Sensing I had no reply for him, he turned around and left the bedroom, slamming the door behind him. Shaken, my insides twisting, I returned to Mount Zion.

* * *

Outside King David's Tomb I am startled by the blinding afternoon light. The Ministry of Tourism has not provided a drinking fountain, nor do I hear the word of the Lord, unless that word is *water*, which is clearly coming from inside me. How can the word of the Lord come from inside me? I turn to Vilnay's book for guidance.

Various buildings surround King David's Tomb. In the cellar of one is the Chamber of the Martyrs (*Martef HaShoah*), dedicated to the memory of the millions of Jews who were slaughtered by the Nazis in the Second World War.

A cellar sounds inviting in this heat. Death is in the air. At least in the chamber it will be cooler than under the unforgiving sun. Maybe I will stay there until sunset since there is no hope for water. Among the empty stone buildings I find a small black guidepost next to five descending stairs signposted "Cave of Remembrance." I walk down the stairs, thinking how far I am from Shaker Square, Woolworth's, and Howard Johnson's. I wouldn't mind a vanilla milkshake or a double scoop of fudge ripple right now. How rocky, gray, and desolate Jerusalem is compared to my verdant Ann Arbor, where I am one year away from graduation, how melancholy compared to Shaker Heights, the Valley of God's Pleasure.

A dark wooden door opens easily with one push. I enter a cave, cool as an ice-skating rink. The shift from heat to cold, from light to darkness is so abrupt it takes me several minutes to adjust. I feel my way around the walls of the cave with my hands. At each step, my startled hands touch a cool metal plaque and my fingers read: 1938–1944, 1939–1943, 1941–1945, 1942–1944. Below each date is a name. I cannot make out the names because they are all in Hebrew, the ancient tongue I do not know.

Even in the light I cannot read Hebrew. The dead children remain nameless.

That's when God whispers in my ear two words in the imperative voice: *Come back.* August 3, 1966. Cave of Remembrance, Mount Zion, Jerusalem. Noonish.

Come back, he whispers. *Come back.*

I run out of the cave breathing heavily, chased by a spectral voice. Facing east toward the Dead Sea, I force myself to remember who I am (Judy, daughter of Rita and Neal), where I come from (Cleveland), and why I must return to Ann Arbor (one more year of college).

I cover my ears with tense hands.

Come back, the voice insists. I assume it is telling me to return to Jerusalem, for the voice knows I will be leaving Israel at the end of August for the United States. The voice wants me to come back to Mount Zion.

My body contracts into itself, elbows piercing my stomach, fists banging my forehead. Shame, guilt, and ignorance overwhelm me. When I look at the entrance sign again, I see part of this cave is dedicated to the memory of Jewish children who were gassed and cremated during the Holocaust.

With no father nearby, I berate myself. I know Latin, French, and Old English, but I cannot read the Hebrew names of children burned in the Holocaust. Hitler has succeeded in wiping out the Jewish people, I tell myself, thirsty and tired, ashamed and confused. I bend over and moan. If I can't keep the memory of these children alive, I am complicit in their deaths. The moan turns into a cry and a sentence: guilty.

The unforgiving sun batters my bare head and blinds me, so I return to the Cave of Remembrance. I touch each plaque again and whisper, "I'm sorry. I am so sorry. I will not forget you." By the end of the circle, tears slide down my face like a mighty stream; breath becomes staccato. I turn to the center of the cave and listen. The voice returns: *Come back. Come back.*

I turn in circles but find nothing. *Come back*, it repeats, this time even softer, and I, anxious to silence it altogether, say, "Yes. Yes, I will return." I vow to come back to Jerusalem for a year. I will learn the names of dead children so that they did not die in vain.

I have never made a vow, and such a vow is by no means natural for a lover of English. English is my homeland. I write, therefore I am. I write college papers on Jonathan Winthrop and the American Revolution, Hart Crane and the American dream, Oneida and American utopianism. I hated afternoon Hebrew school. All I learned was *hineni*, to confirm my presence in the classroom. Nonetheless, in the Cave of Remembrance I vow to devote one academic year to the guttural, archaic, backward language.

Exhausted from this bizarre visit, I dry my eyes on my bare arms and leave the cave, wondering if this is the work of the Lord.

I wobble down Mount Zion, dying for water. Without opening Vilnay I sense from the depth of my soul where I am going, for I have been called. Come, says the Lord. Let us go up. Not for just an hour. Not for one August afternoon, but for a year. Let us learn the language and read the names of dead children.

* * *

My book on Canaanite cults was resting on my chest. When I heard Elliot turn off the television in the living room, I put the book facedown on the floor, turned off my reading lamp, and pretended to sleep. What kept me awake was a question. Why, even though I had come back to Jerusalem and learned enough Hebrew to read those names, why, even though I had stayed not one year but sixteen and had no intention of leaving, why, even though I could walk to Mount Zion in thirty minutes, why had I never returned to read those names?

Chapter Five: Breakthrough

Two weeks after the Passover vacation, my waiting for a reply from Rabbi Green came to an end. His letter arrived in a white envelope, a US Airmail stamp on the upper right corner and the address of Temple Emanu El embossed on the upper left. As my fingers traced the embossed letters I thought of the bar and bat mitzvah, confirmation, and dancing school invitations I had received as an adolescent in Shaker Heights, along with fancy invitations to hayrides and formal dances. How my life had changed. Now I lived with six other Jewish families in a four-story stone building built by Arabs in 1929 in Jerusalem's Bak'a neighborhood. My neighbors in the building hailed from Rhodes, Yemen, Morocco, and the Jewish Quarter of the Old City of Jerusalem. Elliot and I, Canadian and American, and our three sabra children lived on the top floor of this haphazard ingathering of the exiles.

The original Arab owners had built the house for their extended family, but during Israel's 1948 War of Independence, the family fled to Ramallah, expecting to return to Bak'a, an Arab neighborhood during the British Mandate, as soon as the Zionists were vanquished. Only in late June of 1967, after the Six-Day War, did a man from Ramallah knock on the doors of the apartments at 41 Bethlehem Road. According to my downstairs neighbor, Shoshana, he was the son of the man who had built the house and he wanted to see the property his family had lost. Shoshana, born in the Old City, understood the pull to one's past and let him in. Together they sat at her table and drank mint tea with sugar, talked about displacement and war, and then the man rose and left, never to be seen again.

When Elliot and I moved into the building in 1972, the hallway with its sixty-four stairs leading to our apartment had no lighting. Red and black electrical wires do-si-doed along peeling beige walls. The peels fell on the stairs like shards from the contested past. Weeds, deeply entrenched, like ideologies, covered the garden adjacent to the entrance. Neighborhood drug addicts occasionally sat on the stairs in the entrance hall. It was into our metal mailbox, hanging precariously from one nail in this entrance hall, that the fateful letter from Rabbi Green arrived. I had just returned from the bakery at the corner of Bethlehem Road and Judah, where Avraham always gave me a warm, moist rugelach, an act that convinced me to buy more rugelach. The air outside was as warm as the bag of pastries in my hands. Buds of jasmine and pomegranates were showing on the trees along the street, announcing the season of renewal.

I clutched the letter and climbed the stairs. I walked into our sunlit kitchen and put the bag of pastries in the bread drawer. How I loved that view of Jerusalem from the kitchen window, looking west over the Refaim Valley. Isosceles triangles of pines dotted the landscape between rectangles of beige, pink, and white Jerusalem stone. Hills rose and fell in gentle repose toward the white Jerusalem Theater in the distance, and on the horizon the white tower of the Hilton Hotel declared its position of sentinel of modernity.

I thought of burning the letter rather than opening it. The act would be easy and would certainly please Elliot and the children. Or I could fold it into an airplane and fly it out the window. It might get squished by the number six bus. Maybe the dirty sheep that grazed in the open lot across the street would chew it to smithereens. Thus, I could continue living with questions.

I lifted the chicken scissors from the silverware drawer and sliced open the envelope, carried the letter to the TV swivel chair in the living room, and sat down to read.

Dear Judy:

I am having great difficulty in trying to answer your questions. I have a recollection of which I am not altogether certain: an image in my mind of being with your dad at the cemetery and saying some brief prayers. If that was so, they probably were the 23rd psalm and a brief composition of my own and perhaps the Kaddish.

There is no record at Berkowitz-Kumin Funeral Directors, and the related undertakers (they are all together now) of any service for Joseph Stonehill, or any other record of him there. I communicated with the City of Cleveland. They will respond to your letter only if you have the exact date, which I do not have. (Their address is Bureau of Statistics, City Hall, 601 Lakeside Ave. Cleveland, OH 44114). Otherwise you can come down personally and search their records on Thursdays or Fridays 8:30 to 4:00.

I imagine the City of Akron has similar rules. I keep wondering where other records might be. I will pursue these and if I come up with anything helpful I will surely communicate with you. It just may be that you'll have to ask your folks more, but that is your decision, for I am certainly keeping this confidential.

When will you be back in Cleveland? I would so like to see you.

All my love,

Alan S. Green

The letter sat on my lap. My brain played duck, duck, goose. Here was a man, much kinder and nicer than I could have imagined, who was trying to give me back my past. I did have a baby brother. Maybe. He died. Perhaps. The rabbi's letter confirmed this possibility, though the wording—"I am not altogether certain . . . If that was so . . . probably . . . perhaps . . . There is no record"—left room for doubt and conjecture.

Rabbi Green gave me names and addresses so that I could pursue my research. But he also left enough doubt so that I could fantasize. If there was no record of Joseph Stonehill at the funeral home, maybe my brother was still alive. The rabbi did not remember the house call, but can you expect a rabbi to remember all the house calls he makes? Or all the funerals over which he presides?

Granted, it was strange that for the funeral at which he might have officiated my mother was absent. What was she doing that day? Getting a manicure? How could there be no record from any undertaker of my baby brother?

Rabbi Green wanted to see me. I made a note to myself to visit him during my next trip to Cleveland, because here was a man who had helped me understand that I was only at the beginning of my search, not the end.

Rabbi Green's letter gave me hope: I was on a mission in the real world. Like Lewis and Clark, I held in my hands a trail of mappable space. Soon I would discover, perhaps, my lost past. Eventually, maybe, I could fill the hole in my history.

Temple Emanu El

2200 SOUTH GREEN ROAD
CLEVELAND, OHIO 44121

ALAN S. GREEN, D.D., D.H.L., Rabbi

Dear Judy:

I am having great difficulty in trying to answer
your questions. I have a recollection of which I am not
altogether certain: an image in my mind of being with your
dad at the cemetery and saying some brief prayers. If that
was so they probably were the 23rd psalm and a brief composition of my own and perhaps the kaddish.

There is no record at Berkowitz-Kumin Funeral
Directors, and the related undertakers (they are all together
now) of any service for George Joseph Stonehill, or any other
record of him there.

I communicated with the City of Cleveland. They
will respond to your letter only if you have the exact date,
which I do not have. (Their Address is Bureau of Statistics
City Hall, 601 Lakeside Ave. Cleveland, OH 44114).
Otherwise you can come down personally and search their records
on Thursdays or Fridays 8:30 to 4:00.

I imagine the City of Akron has similar rules.

I keep wondering where other records might be.
I will pursue these and if I come up with anything
helpful I will surely communicate with you. It just may be
that you'll have to ask your folks more, but that is your
decision, for I am certainly keeping this confidential.

When will you be back in Cleveland? I would so
like to see you.

                    All my love,

                    Alan S. Green

Chapter Six: Making Room

After a year or so of reading and rereading Rabbi Green's letter, a certain boldness began to take root inside me. I could almost imagine calling my mother again and asking for details. Each time I contemplated the call, though, I felt like I had to clean out my apartment. As I threw out all my college books about the American Revolution, I realized I would never become a scholar of the eighteenth-century idea of America as the New Jerusalem. I began to accept the fact that I had been living in the old Jerusalem for seventeen years, my three children born here, registered in the city's mediocre schools, my chicken and vegetables purchased in its markets, my fears stemming from its wars and terror. The act of throwing away the old books and dreams helped root me in the present.

I wanted to become more *hineni*, here, in the present.

But hesitancy persisted, so I cleaned out the children's closets. With each child, I spent three healthy afternoons fingering, folding, and throwing away their pasts: single socks, T-shirts stained with tomato sauce, blue jeans torn and mended until there was nothing left to wear without using paper clips.

Boldness growing, but still not ready, I cleaned out my own closet. I prepared two bulging garbage bags full of shawls, skirts, shoes, and winter hats for new immigrants from Ethiopia and Russia who had arrived in Israel with nothing more than the shirts on their backs.

As immigrants we all shared the difficult task of defining who we were in a new homeland. What did we need in the present, and what could we throw out from the past? The stronger I became rooted in the present, the louder I said *hineni*, I am here! Soon I was fortified to confront my mother. One night, when it was ten o'clock in Jerusalem and three in the afternoon in Sarasota, Florida, where my mother and father now lived permanently, I sat on my bed and dialed. Our bedroom door was locked because I did not want to be disturbed. Fortunately, my mother answered the phone.

"Hi, sweetheart. How's the weather over there?"

"The weather's beautiful, Mom. We had a warm, dry Chanukah."

An uncomfortable silence grew, the kind I usually filled with stories about the children—Joseph's precocious gymnastic escapades, Miriam's violin lessons, Michael's first hike in the Negev. I took a deep breath.

"Mom, I have a request."

"What is it, dear?"

At that moment, Elliot started knocking on the door. I jumped off the bed and ran to open it. "Why are you locking me out of my room?" he asked, sounding hurt. Before I could explain, he said in a voice even the neighbors could hear, "Who the fuck do you think you are?"

I covered the receiver with one hand and told him I was talking to my mother in Sarasota.

"I don't give a shit who you're talking to, asshole." He stomped out of the room and slammed the door.

"What is it, dear?" my mother repeated.

I took a deep breath. "I've been thinking about Joey again, a lot, lately."

"You mean . . . the baby? Your brother? . . . It's balmy down here in Florida."

"Yes. My brother. Of course I am not my brother's keeper, but I'd like to know what happened." Where did that come from?

Fortunately, my mother ignored it. Her tone switched from stereotypical cheer to hesitancy. "I can't imagine why you're thinking about that now . . ."

"I don't know, Mom. It haunts me. I cry. Feel sad sometimes . . ."

"Well. I'll try to collect my thoughts, dear," she said. "I'll write you. What are you serving for dinner?"

I told her it was ten o'clock at night and the children were in bed. I felt kindly toward her and understood her need for avoidance. Hadn't we all avoided the topic for decades? Weren't we all champion avoiders, gold-star deniers, late bloomers?

"You must be tired," she said. "Why don't we talk another time."

I took a deep breath and thanked her and said I was looking forward to her letter. I was grateful she didn't ask anything about Elliot. Perhaps we were avoiding this too.

What success! I had asked my mother for help and she did not deny the past. I walked into the living room, where Elliot was reading the evening newspaper and watching a political commentary talk show during which all four panelists were shouting at each other at the same time. I wanted to apologize about the locked door, explain, and tell him about my milestone conversation with my mother, but his frozen, stiff chest told me nobody was home. Again, stretching for facts across the ocean was followed by an inner excitement. Soon I would have all the details, and my obsession with the past, this compulsive retrospection, would dissolve. I would be free, filled with energy to love and cuddle my own children and work on loving my husband.

But during that liminal waiting time, ghosts came back.

Chapter Seven: Ghosts

The Day Tweety Dies

Mom buys a pet bird in a Cleveland basement pet shop right before *The Ed Sullivan Show*. The bird tweets in a silver cage in the corner of the green breakfast room. The family names the bird Tweety. The family talks to Tweety, simple sentences like "Hi, Tweety" and "Hey, Tweety," and Tweety tweets back. When Tweety tweets, everyone's happy.

Sometimes I feel sorry for Tweety because he's locked in a cage.

One day Tweety flies out the front door of his cage while Vashti, the maid, is feeding him seeds. Tweety heads straight for the window above the kitchen sink and bumps into the glass again and again. Nobody knows what to do. Tweety wants the wild, wide spaces where parakeets sing to each other.

Everyone's helpless, including Vashti.

Tweety falls onto the edge of the kitchen sink and from there collapses onto the gray linoleum floor. He looks like an abused pancake, soft and bruised.

I didn't know you could be dead without bleeding.

"Clean up the goddamn mess," Daddy yells.

Nobody tweets during the evening stew. While I swallow green beans and milk, silence nibbles at me from inside, enlarging the hole that's already there.

I loved Tweety. If there was ever a happy family day, it was when Tweety sang in his cage and everyone passed the mashed potatoes.

The Day Hat Dies

Oy vey! Oy vey! Mom's beauty shop burns down in Shaker Square. What a close call. Oy vey! Mom's still alive, but her favorite hat—the brown felt one with white-and-beige feathers on the side—is dead. Burnt. Charred to ash.

Mom mourns that hat by talking about it at breakfast and dinner. It was such a beautiful hat. The way the white-and-beige feathers echoed her frosted brown hair and highlighted her gray-green eyes. That hat made Mom look like a queen.

She tells the story again for dessert. "It was such a close call. I can't tell you how scared I was. I was reading *House Beautiful* under the dryer, so of course I couldn't hear anything. The room filled with smoke, and suddenly everyone in the beauty shop was running around like crazy. I pushed up the dryer—it was so heavy—and asked Tony what happened. 'Fire! Fire!' he screamed. I didn't see the flames, just all the women running around like crazy. Tony didn't know what to grab first—his appointment book or color chart.

"'My hat! My hat!' I cried. 'I can't leave without my hat.'

"'There's no time for that, Rita,' Tony yelled. 'You must come now.'

"So I ran out of the beauty shop into the arcade and then to the parking lot, with my hair in curlers. Can you imagine? Standing in the parking lot with my hair in curlers! And my hat, my beautiful little brown felt hat with the white-and-beige feathers was left inside and burned."

Mom's tears make dots the size of chocolate chips in the vanilla junket. She will remember that hat forever.

Whenever she wears some hat that is not ideal, she says, "Do you remember that hat I had when Tony was at the old place? You know, the one that burned."

The Day Three Fish Die

I walk with Elizabeth to Woolworth's at Shaker Square. She carries the money because she is ten. We stand next to the aquariums and stare for a long time. Fish swim in circles. Am I a fish? No, I am a snail. Curled into myself, I choke on my own breath. Turtles climb, one leg at a time, onto the checkerboard backs of their friends. They cost only twenty-five cents. I want one, but don't say. Elizabeth wants three goldfish, and says. That's what we buy.

I can't say what I want. Maybe they don't sell it at Woolworth's. Or at Hough Bakery. I never saw it in the children's department on the second floor of Franklin Simon. I looked in the Colony Drug but didn't see it there. I don't know what it is because I've never seen it, so how can I find it? But something is missing, and it's tied to my breath and the deep hole inside.

Ten days later the three goldfish die. Vashti flushes the yucky water and fish. "They're goin' down to Toilet Heaven," she says.

Ghosts spook the castle house.

One bird ghost, one hat ghost, three goldfish ghosts, and a ghost named Joey.

Chapter Eight: "Facts and Events"

My mother's letter arrived when the country was ablaze with the scandal about the General Security Services after it came to light that it had been responsible for killing two Palestinian terrorists after they had been taken alive two years earlier, in 1984. The two terrorists, along with two others, had hijacked Egged bus number 300, which had been carrying forty-one passengers from Tel Aviv to Ashkelon. The Israeli censor had tried to cover up the scandalous murders. The truth came out in dribs and dabs. In addition to the head of the GSS being forced to leave his position, inflation in Israel was nearing three hundred percent. But neither the economic nor the political urgencies of the day fazed me, for I was on a mission.

In my hands I held my mother's letter—five pieces of yellow paper torn from a legal pad. Thin turquoise lines kept the words in order. My mother's thoughts had been written down with a blue ballpoint pen in a staccato script full of dashes and fierce dots. Each sentence marked a stop along my journey, each word a rare gift drudged from the past, dear as moon rock. This was as close as I would ever get to the truth about my baby brother.

While the children slept, I crawled under the covers of my bed and dove into the black hole of my childhood. Fortunately, Elliot was sleeping in front of the TV. Fortunately, too, a box of tissues stood ready next to my bed.

Dear Judy,

I have been collecting the facts and events you inquired about and shall try to recall the best I can all about our little family from June 1948, when we moved to 2849 Ludlow, to November 21, 1951, when your brother Jimmy happily for all of us arrived.

My pregnancy, my third attended by the same physician who delivered both you and Elizabeth, Dr. W. R. Freund, when I was 27–28 years old—was not going well. I had a toxic pregnancy - - symptoms - - high blood pressure and albumin in the urine. I believe I was to rest somewhat and always being a good patient I followed the Doctor's orders diligently.

Elizabeth started kindergarten Fall '48 and you went to Miss Brunner's nursery school. That was the time of Vashti - - with the "fanny spoon" and cigarette holder. Do you remember her? She was an exceptional person, housekeeper and great with both my precious daughters.

Then it happened - - I delivered one month early - - June 18, 1949, at McDonald House; baby boy Stonehill - - 6 lbs. some oz. - - - Somewhere during or after delivery - - poor little thing suffered an irreversible cerebral hemorrhage, but the vital organs appeared satisfactory.

I expected the sky to fall, or an earthquake to hit Jerusalem again, or at least the clock next to my bed to stop ticking, but at the moment of truth, nothing major occurred. The moment of reading passed, like other moments. No volcano erupted inside me, though I sensed a shift, an immeasurable turning toward light. This turning, more like the opening of an air passage, was accompanied by a relaxation of my stomach muscles, which I then noticed had been tense. My breathing grew deeper as I continued to read.

> We called Rabbi Green - - who was out of the city - - and Rabbi Earl Stone, who was at The Temple, came to see us. He now has been in Denver, Col., all these years and most coincidentally was the Rabbi who performed H's conversion. The only person who visited in the Hospital besides the family was Harry Fiterman, who happened to be attending his Bellfaire meeting then. I think it was his very first visit to Cleveland and he was really the only one to see the beautiful newborn. And he was beautiful - - fair haired and exquisite blue eyes.

I needed a tissue. I knew the delicacy and vulnerability of a mother looking at her first son, how she marvels at the perfection of his face, hands, body. I let my tears come before I returned to reading.

> Our pediatrician then, Dr. Seymour Kyman, was not encouraging, nor were any of the other medical people. - - But Dad and I always had a lot of hope. Sometime later - - I don't really know at what age - - we finally brought home George Joseph Stonehill, whom we all called Joey.

Unfortunately - - it's doubtful he ever heard his name or anything else - - nor ever could see out of his beautiful eyes. - - The neurologist Dr. Siegfried Baumoel & all others used the term *vegetable* to describe him. - - When we brought him home I promised myself - - I would buy a certain pair of silver candlesticks - - which I indeed did, sort of a commemoration.

The middle bedroom with the red farm scene wallpaper became his room - - the one that had been yours. We started with a practical nurse - - there was no schedule and he cried & fussed a great deal. Dad was wonderful with him, and after the nurse left he took care of the night feedings. It was sometime during this episode - - or later on - - I do not recall the exact time - - that Grandma came to live with us, accepting the invitation of her son-in-law. Our household sure was busy.

We became involved with an organization in support of Cerebral Palsy and looked for anything & everything we thought would help. He did gain - - although quite slowly, and every now and then we thought he responded to light. But it really was all wishful thinking and really no improvement. Little Joey was taking all parental time and unfortunately showing absolutely no improvement. Sometime in early winter or spring 1950 [*sic*] was one of the saddest days in our life. Arrangements were made to have little Joey cared for in a private home setting by people specializing in care for special babies. The Doctor told us this type of infant usually does not live very long and life expectancy is very limited. The sight of your Dad carrying our beautiful but helpless son in our wicker laundry basket, bundled up in his colorful blankets, taking him to his new home outside Akron, Ohio - - was & still is the very lowest, saddest time of our life. I shall always admire his (Dad's) physical & emotional strength that particular day.

I had to eat something, take a break. Perhaps I would read the last page the next day, or in a month, or a year. There were so many details to digest—more facts than I could handle. What would I do with these facts, with my mother's honesty, with her loving tone that was so different from the superficial one I was accustomed to in our phone conversations and in my imagination?

I tried to fall asleep but was visited by words, not dreams. My mother's phrases filled my head like mantras: "I have been collecting the facts . . . Then it happened . . .

And he was beautiful . . . all others used the term *vegetable* . . . Our household sure was busy . . . it really was all wishful thinking . . . The sight of your dad . . ." Close to midnight my husband came into the room and went to sleep. His breathing warmed me. I wanted to hug him but didn't. I fell asleep to the words "wishful thinking."

The next morning, after the children left for pre-K and school and Elliot for work, I sat down at the dining room table and finished the letter.

> Now - - we could give you girls the time and attention that had been lacking these many months. I don't know if you or Elizabeth felt neglected during that period - - but you had just cause and at ages 3 and 5 certainly could not understand.
>
> In February 1951, we were called that George Joseph Stonehill died from Pneumonia. You do recall Rabbi Green came to talk to all of us and lead us in prayers. We had no funeral and there was no burial - - cremation, I think. As I look back - - it appears obvious we wanted to forget the sadness - - but we'll never really forget "Joey."
>
> God was very good to us - - 9 ½ months later James Neal arrived, 2 weeks before my 30th birthday. Sometime - - & I'm not

certain exactly - - I think Spring 1950 - - I fell apart; was treated by the neurologist, Dr. Siegfried Baumoel; and after a series of electric shock treatments I picked up all the pieces and got on with the business of caring for my wonderful family.

Thurs. A.M. - - I think this covers everything pretty well - - honey. I've tried to fill in this portion of your young life; always ask if there is something from the past you want to know. If I can help - - will do. Dad also is well tuned in - - for sure even better than I in most areas. - - Take care - - Honey - - The best is yet to come - - Now we'll concentrate on your's and your gorgeous families [*sic*] future - --

Love always,

Mom

neurologist, Dr. Siegfried Baumoel, and after a series of electric shock treatments I picked up all the pieces and got on with the business of caring for my wonderful family.

Thurs. A.M.   I think this covers everything pretty well - honey. I've tried to fill in the pattern of your young life. Always ask if there is something from the past you want to know. If I can help - will do. Dad also is well tuned in -- ~~for sure~~ even better than I in most areas. -

Take care - Honey - The best is yet to come - Now we'll concentrate on your's and your gorgeous families future

Love always
Mom

Chapter Nine: The Outrageous Fiction, Lillian

For months I read and reread my mother's letter. Once I mastered reading it without crying, I decided to write to the Bureau of Statistics in Cleveland to ask for a death certificate.

"If you have nothing on file for George Joseph Stonehill, born June 18, 1949, could you please forward this request to the appropriate address in Akron?" I wrote. "Perhaps his death is registered there."

Two months later I received an efficient no-nonsense typed letter from the Akron Health Department. That day, Joseph, with an older friend, performed gymnastic exercises for pocket money in front of the Mashbir department store in downtown Jerusalem, Miriam gave a violin recital, and Michael got an A on his science project on volcanoes. All this paled next to the skimpy piece of paper from Akron, Ohio.

> Judy,
>
> We have a George Joseph Stonehill, age 1 that died 2-24-51. He died at the Woody Haven Boarding Home of Congenital Spastic Paralysis. If you would like a copy of the death record, a certified copy is $7.00. An uncertified copy is $2.50. File No. 423-51.
>
> Please remit in cash, check or money order made payable to the City of Akron.
>
> Akron Health Dept.
> Vital Records
> 177 S. Broadway St.
> Akron, OH 44308

How do you prepare for the arrival of a death certificate for a brother you barely remember but whose ghost whispers and causes tears decades after his death? Do you cover mirrors, avoid music, and wear black? After

I sent the Akron Health Department of Vital Statistics a check for seven dollars, and while waiting for the document to arrive, my imagination reigned. Lillian, like a loving mother from the land of salvation, emerged fully formed and ready to help.

How Lillian Saved Joey

Lillian, one of the paramedics over at Woody Haven, worked nights. She was forty-four and lived by herself in a two-room bungalow within walking distance of Woody Haven. She had never married. Born and raised an Akron girl, the farthest she ever wandered from home was Sandusky, for a Fourth of July picnic at her aunt's place, when she was thirty. "Got everything I need right here," she'd tell her cronies at work when they'd share tales of trips to Las Vegas and Orlando. "All I need is these children," she'd say, picking up a bundle to burp.

Something about Joey's blue eyes attracted her. But it wasn't just the astounding color that drew her in. No, this little one had intelligence. She could feel it when she'd pick him up and put him on her shoulder. "Swing low, sweet chariot," she'd sing to him, and when he was fussing and couldn't get to sleep, she'd sing the slow version of "This Little Light of Mine." While other babies his age with fewer problems lay in their cribs like so much lettuce, Joey seemed more like a carrot, granted a limp carrot, but a carrot nonetheless. After ten or twenty minutes of singing, he'd hold his head erect as if he were a normal baby, as if he had no intention whatsoever of going to sleep this night, or any night, as if he were saying to the world, which at the time was only Lillian's shoulder and warm chest, *I want to see. Name the world for me. Let me touch and feel. Give me something to smell. Sing louder. I want to live!*

It was uncanny, Lillian thought, how such a baby (well, he wasn't such a baby anymore, he was already one and a half; soon he'd be sitting up and then walking, if he got the right kind of help) with so many problems, right from birth, still had that inner urge to live. It was a mystery, that urge. She saw it in some babies, and it didn't matter what diagnosis they came in with. They wanted to live, even though their hearts or brains, or sometimes their kidneys, were pulling them down, back into the dust from which came the whole human race, those with functioning brains and those without. Most of the people she knew outside Woody Haven had functioning brains but nevertheless lacked that spark of life that she felt in every inch of skin on this little boy's body.

After fifteen years on the job she trusted her instincts. Why, she had seen babies come to Woody Haven directly from the hospital without even going home to their parents and families, and also babies who stayed home for a month or five or ten and then came out here all the way to Akron, sometimes from as far away as Cincinnati, because the parents collapsed under the demands of caring for what the doctors called "vegetable" babies. Those doctors, they always predicted the baby would be dead within six months, no matter how old the babies were when they arrived. Of course, the same doctors never showed up at the child's third birthday at Woody Haven. And good thing they didn't. They didn't deserve to see what miracles some twenty-four/seven TLC could bring. Vegetables, my ass. These children just needed a bosom and a song. Doctors weren't prophets, even though they liked to play that role. Lillian knew that, and she also knew that Joey was a good bet.

It was just about the time that Joey came to Woody Haven that Lillian's father passed and she began to feel lonely. Her father had spent the last year of his life in the old folks' home after she couldn't lift him no more. She had visited him every day, either before or after work. Now that he had passed, Lillian felt sad every day. She had no one. Sure there was Will out in Kansas, but she couldn't even pronounce the name of the town where he lived, let alone go visit there. The bus ride to Sandusky had been enough to convince her that if you can't walk somewhere, it ain't worth going.

Each day she dreaded waking up in an empty house with no one to take care of until the night shift started at four. She believed with all her soul she was born to mother and nurture, only God had played a dirty trick on her.

The plan came to her one Friday night at the end of her shift, just before midnight. It was so simple she stood stock still in the little kitchen, dazzled by its clarity. She signed out, on that cold January night in 1951, at 12:03. Then she walked into the room where Joey was sleeping in his crib. A blue-and-white quilt with yellow ducks covered him, the same quilt he had come in with three weeks earlier. She lifted the quilt and then lifted the baby onto her shoulder, covering him again nice and tight with the quilt. She took another woolen blanket from the cupboard and covered him with that too. It was freezing outside, and the weatherman said it would get even colder tomorrow. She didn't want the little thing to catch pneumonia, like so many of the poor babies did.

Lillian left through the back door, like she did every night. The place was quiet and still; nobody saw her. Still, too, was the street outside, the sidewalks covered with snow, each star in the sky twinkling, as if saying, *Take me, take me.* Light from the streetlamps lit her way. The half mile to her house felt like a pilgrimage to some holy land where she would find love and redemption. The colder the wind blew, the warmer she felt in her heart. She vowed to keep this child warm and loved for as long as she could.

At home she put Joey down on her corduroy couch in the living room and placed pillows around him, the same pillows that had given support to her father. She walked around the coffee table, keeping her eyes on little Joey, and put two logs in the fireplace. When they were burning well, she unwrapped Joey and took off his pajamas. He sure was small for his age. All those wrappings made him look heftier, but in truth he was no bigger than a bundle of fresh sweetcorn. His arms were limp as leftover french fries, his legs slim, with no chubby rings like those on other little boys his age. But the part that most astonished Lillian, that actually made her gasp on that January night, was his little penis. She had seen it before, changing him at night, thinking nothing of its small size, but now she understood. The little thing was cut half off! It looked like the tail of a baby turtle.

"Dear God," she said, her breath quivering, "he's a Hebrew." She grabbed her Holy Bible from the coffee table and with one hand on the bible and the other on Joey, prayed to the God of Abraham, Isaac, and Jacob. "Give me strength, dear Lord, both physical and spiritual, to raise this little Hebrew boy in the paths of righteousness, that he may know Your loving kindness and mercy, and that he may never forget his great ancestry and always walk proud, if he walks at all, as a man of the House of Abraham. Amen, amen."

After that first night it was clear as God's love how they would spend their waking time together during the day, before they went to Woody Haven. She would train him to sleep when she slept, and every day she massaged his legs and arms with peanut oil. While she rubbed, Lillian told Joey Bible stories. She started with creation and worked her way through Cain and Abel, the Tower of Babel, Noah and the flood, Abraham and Sarah. She spent long hours on the Joseph saga and the Exodus from

Egypt. She had heard these stories from her mother, who had heard them from her mother, who had grown up a slave in Georgia. Whenever a hymn or song seemed appropriate to the story, Lillian sang. She sang about the baby in the bulrushes, crossing the Jordan River, and the beautiful Promised Land. She did not hold back any words from this little child, and when he cried and fussed, she held him on her bosom and hummed until they both fell asleep.

With all her kneading and massaging of Joey's limbs, by his second birthday he was able to sit.

The folks at Woody Haven couldn't believe what she was doing. In the beginning Dr. Small, whom everyone on staff called Smallballs behind his back, was furious. "You can't just take a child home like that, Lillian. You know that. It's . . . it's against the law."

"And you know he'll die at Woody Haven," Lillian said, "just like all the rest of them. At least with me, Doc, he'll have a chance. He's special, Doc. I know he can grow."

A retired pediatrician from Canton, Dr. Small didn't like the arrangement. "What will we tell the parents?"

What did they tell all the parents, those who took an interest? Most of them never even called, let alone visited. There were parents who, when notified that their babies had died, didn't even bother to take care of the funeral arrangements. "Tell them he got pneumonia and died," she said. "I know it sounds cruel, but it's not so far-fetched."

Small nodded.

Lillian was amazed at his agreement, totally out of character and against the law. "Lillian, if the police get wind of this, you know we're finished," he said. "Woody Haven will turn into a parking lot and we'll all lose our jobs." He watched Lillian as she turned over some other babies. "Tell me something," he said, watching her work. "Why?"

"Why what?" Guilt and love scrambled in her heart.

"Why this one?" he said. "Why are you setting yourself up for disappointment? You know he'll never make it."

Lillian looked at him as if he were not a two-legged creature created in the image of God but a specimen of a different species. "Doc," she said, covering a little girl and rubbing her head, "I want to love one baby, love him completely . . . all day, not just on the night shift." He turned away as she continued. "I want to feel needed . . . This is the one I've chosen."

Small walked out of the room, shaking his head in disbelief, and murmuring, "Chosen," as if it were some crazy foreign word.

The next day Lillian called Mr. Billow, over at Billow's Funeral Homes and Crematory. She told him that one of their babies at Woody Haven, a George Joseph Stonehill from up in Cleveland, had died of pneumonia. She would send over all the information so he could fill out the legal forms. Dr. Small would take the body to Cleveland that day, since he was going up there for another case. "He's a Jewish baby, Mr. Billow, so the doctor will take the body to Deutsch Funeral Home."

Because the folks at Billow's worked closely with Woody Haven, they had no reason to doubt Lillian's story. Whatever she told them was fine. One less tragedy to deal with. Lillian asked that they just notify the family, a Mr. and Mrs. Neal Stonehill, which they did on a Sunday night. They told Mr. Stonehill that Dr. Small took the body to Deutsch Funeral Home and that Mr. Stonehill could be in touch with Deutsch directly if he wanted. Otherwise, Deutsch would take care of everything. Both Woody Haven and Billow's knew that most of the families wanted to forget, deny, and repress the birth of a special child. They would do whatever it took to erase the tragedy from their lives.

Lillian raised Joey as if he were her own flesh and blood. By his fifth birthday he could crawl and pull himself up to a standing position. By his seventh he was walking with crutches. Though he couldn't see Lillian, he felt the warmth of her love. It radiated throughout their small house, in her words, her voice and touch, her smell, her every breath. He smiled whenever she entered the room. He learned to hug.

Chapter Ten: Never Coming Back

The Certificate of Death arrived. When I held it in my hands, I knew Joey was never coming back.

I did the math. Joey lived at Woody Haven for forty-five days. That meant my father had taken him there on January 10, 1951. If I assumed Joey came home four months after his birth—on October 28, 1949 (when I was four and a quarter years old)—and left on January 10, 1951, he and I lived together on Ludlow Road for 439 days. More than fourteen months.

From the Certificate of Death I learned that my Single White American Male brother, who had no occupation or business and who never served in the armed forces and didn't have a social security number, was one year, eight months, and six days old at time of death (6:15 a.m.) on February 24, 1951.

Rubric 18, "Cause of Death," raised questions. Whoever signs the document is instructed to enter the disease, condition, injury, complication, or condition directly leading to death on line (a). Line (b) is for the morbid conditions, if any, giving rise to (a). On line (c) whoever signs the document is asked to write the name of other significant conditions contributing to the death but not related to the disease or condition causing death.

From my mother's letter I understood that the disease directly leading to death was pneumonia, but the Certificate of Death states congenital spastic paralysis. It seemed to me that congenital spastic paralysis should have appeared on line (b) or (c).

These three words—*congenital spastic paralysis*—also made my eyebrows rise. What was the implication underlying this statement that Joey's spastic paralysis had been congenital? "Congenital" seemed to put all the responsibility for Joey's vegetative condition on genetics and the mother. Sure enough, the definition in *Webster's New Universal Unabridged Dictionary* confirmed my suspicions.

> Congenital: 1. of or pertaining to a condition present at birth, **whether inherited or caused by the environment, esp. the uterine environment** [emphasis mine]; 2. having by nature a specified character: *a congenital fool*. See **birth defect**.

Naturally, I went to *birth defect*.

> Birth defect: *Pathol*. Any physical, mental or biochemical abnormality present at birth. Also called congenital defect.

This diagnosis made it sound like Joey had been a vegetable in the womb and his condition was not the result of a botched birth. Was this true? My mother's letter said "somewhere during or after delivery" Joey suffered a cerebral hemorrhage. Could it have been that the obstetrician bore some responsibility for Joey's condition? Wasn't he part of "the environment"?

And what was the story behind the facts on the Certificate of Death regarding a Dr. Fred K. Read? He was Joey's attending doctor from January 20, ten days after Joey arrived at Woody Haven, until 6:15 a.m. on February 24. The hospital and my parents had been able to keep Joey alive for almost eighteen months, but Woody Haven, the institution of place of death, and Dr. Read specifically, couldn't keep him alive for more than forty-five days? What kind of haven had Woody Haven provided? And if Dr. F. K. Read was the attending doctor for thirty-five days, how could he also be the registrar, whose signature appears on the bottom line? This document smelled fishy.

Seeing the name of the crematory made me livid. How could a Jewish burial service provide cremation in 1951, six years after the Holocaust? And why didn't they own up to it when Rabbi Green called them? Who had made this macabre choice? Mr. Billow, the funeral director? Deutsch? My parents?

I had thought the Certificate of Death would finally enable me to allow Joey to rest in peace, but the brief text only raised more disturbing questions.

* * *

Why couldn't I let go?

I pondered this question in the evenings, as I cleared the table after dinner and stood rinsing the plates at the kitchen sink. One night, not long after I had received the Certificate of Death, as Michael and Miriam were watching TV, waiting for their father to return home from work, Joseph was practicing his recorder in his bedroom and I was arranging the dinner dishes in our new Princess dishwasher, the words of a popular song from 1951 came to mind. It was a song my parents had often hummed.

> Unforgettable
> That's what you are
> Unforgettable
> Though near or far
> Like a song of love that clings to me
> How the thought of you does things to me

After Elliot came home and shooed the children to bed, another song came back. It had been my favorite when I was nine. My mother used to yell at me from the kitchen to close the door of the upstairs rec room when I practiced it too often and played it too loudly on the piano.

Jimmy kissed me in the springtime
Tommy kissed me in the fall
But I remember only Joey
Joey kissed me not at all.

Chapter Eleven: Belated Letters to Dead Teachers

Miss Goretzka
Kindergarten Teacher
Ludlow School
Shaker Heights, Ohio

Dear Miss Goretzka,

My baby brother disappeared on January 10, 1951, and died on February 24, 1951. Maybe that was the day during rest period when I wet my cot. The snow was so thick it looked like all the branches on the elm next to the bay window wore casts. Do you remember that day?

I was five years, seven months, and thirteen days old on the day Joey died. Maybe that's why I didn't play in the wooden playhouse—I didn't want to play Family. Couldn't play mother, couldn't play sister, never the baby.

Maybe that's why rest period was my favorite part of the day, watching snow fall and bury everything.

I wish I had told you my secret in 1951. I needed an ear, Miss Goretzka. I also could have used a hand on my shoulder or head. A hug would have been good. I needed a room with a door, shelves stacked with tissues, a quiet person sitting on a comfortable chair like in *Goodnight Moon*, a woman not afraid of tears, a person who would have said, "More, Judy. Tell me more. This is important."

I don't know why I never told you the secret, Miss Goretzka. You could have used it for show-and-tell or told the principal and the school nurse. The sky would not have fallen. Right? Baby Joey was kicking inside me, but I couldn't open up.

Thank you for listening now. Better late than never.

Yours since 1951,

Judy

∗ ∗ ∗

Miss Gelsenliter
First-Grade Teacher
Ludlow School
Shaker Heights, Ohio

Dear Miss Gelsenliter,

Remember after Thanksgiving vacation in 1951 when I told Tim in the cloakroom, "My mother had a baby boy"? We were hanging up our winter jackets. Mine was red, his blue with a fuzzy hood. We both wore plaid scarves around our necks. The hooks were like golden claws.

Of course you don't remember that morning, because you were sitting on the teacher's chair in the reading corner, waiting for all of us to take our places. I wish I had been able to say to Tim, to you and the whole class, not in the dark cloakroom, but in the bright classroom that shone with light even on gray days, I wish I had been able to say: "My mother had a baby boy. This one is Jimmy. The first one died. He was Joey." Saying was important, Miss Gelsenliter, because at the end of November we were learning to see. *See Dick. See Jane. See Spot.* Dick and Jane could say, but I could not.

I wish I had known where my first baby brother was. He left without saying goodbye. Was he buried inside me? Were my mother's tears buried inside me?

How could I see? Who could believe?

Dear Miss Gelsenliter, I wish we had learned words like *death* and *sad.* I needed words beyond *See Spot run.*

Life in the book was always glad. At home, even the walls cried.

Couldn't you see, Miss Gelsenliter?

Such a big secret for the shortest girl in first grade. But it's not your fault. How can I blame you if I never opened my mouth?

Thank you for teaching me how to read. First grade was safe for Dick and Jane. You helped me stay in the lines. Maybe it's good, natural, and right that you helped freeze me in place for the sake of civilization. You taught me to stand straight like an *I,* even when I felt like a lowercase *c*. These too are important lessons. One language is better than none.

Yours since 1952,

Judy

Chapter Twelve: No Iowa Corn

I wanted to master Joey's Certificate of Death as I had mastered Emily Dickinson's "I'm Nobody! Who are you?" But the same question kept gnawing at me with each reading: Why cremation?

I decided to visit Rabbi Green during an upcoming family visit to Cleveland and ask him directly.

His legs, wrapped in white bandages to his thighs, hung from a pole over his bed as if they were out to dry. He was in a private room at Mount Sinai Hospital, being treated for phlebitis. His face and bald head competed for whiteness with his legs.

Pink magnolias blossomed below his window, on East Boulevard, but he couldn't see them because he was confined to his bed. When he stretched out his hands to hold mine, my palms remembered his softness. Did he really need legs when he had hands like these? Hands that caressed and contained, hands that expressed so much gentle, secure love. The sunshine streamed into the room, making his bald head shine and illuminating his sweet smile. I felt as though I were in the presence of an angel. At such moments, words become barriers and the cliché—silence is golden—becomes a deep truth. Rabbi Green's hands and smile spoke compassion, understanding, and love. I wondered how long a person had to work on himself to reach such a state. As I felt the tears forming in the corners of my eyes, for reasons I did not understand, the rabbi spoke.

"Could you give me my glasses, Judy?" He spoke kindly and with as much enthusiasm as a man confined to bed, his legs in the air, could muster. "They're on the nightstand somewhere. I want to get a good look at you."

I did not want to remove my hands from his, but I also did not want to seem rude, so I fumbled around the papers and books, found his wire-rimmed glasses, and handed them to him. After he put them on he looked just like the rabbi who had sat on my living room couch thirty-seven years earlier, but without the Iowa corn stalks I had seen then growing out of his head.

I pulled the one chair in the room up to his bed and sat down. Skipping the niceties, for in five minutes the physiotherapist was due, I asked, "How could Jews cremate after Hitler? Isn't it an insult to the memory of those who were gassed and burned?"

He looked at me with a helpless smile. I felt guilty for being so abrupt, for showing a lack of good manners, rushing head on into my agenda, but I needed him to help me, and for all I knew, he could die before answering the deeper question: Why did my parents burn Joey? Cremation denies us, the survivors, a specific place to mourn. I needed a grave, an address. To me and also to my mother, according to her letter, cremation seemed like an attempt to erase Joey's memory. If so, the attempt had failed. Did he believe in erasure?

Rabbi Green's expression changed. He looked conflicted. He breathed deeply, as if he were on a quiz show and felt stumped. The loving smile returned before he opened his mouth. I could learn so much from this man about communication, I thought to myself. When anyone asks a question that sounds more like a demand, or a complaint, smile first. Next, take a deep breath, think, and only then respond. This gives your questioner the feeling that you are saying, Life is complicated, often incomprehensible, but here's an attempt to answer your question.

"Reform Judaism permits cremation," he said. "About twenty-five percent, maybe more, of Reform Jews do it."

"Six years after Hitler?"

"Yes, even then."

"You know about Molech?" I asked, still angry.

He nodded.

"They burned children. God didn't like it."

He wiped his dry lips with the back of his hand. I picked up the tongue depressor wrapped in damp gauze that sat on his bed stand and handed it to him. He used it to wet his lips.

"Judy, you're confused. That's something else entirely," he said, with the kindness of an experienced teacher. "Those children were alive. They were sacrificed." He closed his eyes as if deep in thought while I sat next to him on a chair, feeling stupid for my dumb associations yet grateful for his clarifications. When he opened his eyes he said, "I don't want to go into all the arguments for and against . . . cremation, that is."

For an instant I felt that maybe he agreed with me. Maybe the Reform Rabbi Green, in his heart, took the Orthodox position that cremation is forbidden. *Talk, talk,* I wanted to say, but he looked tired and in a few minutes he would have to exercise his bum legs. I dabbed the depressor in water and wet his lips again.

"Call Sid Deutsch if you want more details," he said, a tiredness in his voice.

Sid Deutsch. "Deutsch Crematory" had appeared on Joey's Certificate of Death. As I stood up to leave, I was aware that this would probably be the last time I would see this loving man who had held my hand while reciting the twenty-third psalm so many years ago. Rabbi Green's whole being, even with his legs bandaged and suspended in the air, communicated compassion and understanding. He turned deep frustration into resignation with a smile. This was a religious stance beyond words, as if the hands that reached out and held, or blessed during the recitation of the priestly blessing, as he had done at my consecration in 1951 and confirmation in 1960, understood the universal, deep need for holding and for touch. *May the Lord bless you and keep you*, I wanted to say to him, to return that beautiful blessing to him. *May the Lord make His face to shine upon you. May the Lord be gracious unto you*, I wanted to whisper. *And bring you peace.*

Instead, I asked if Deutsch was still in business.

"Yes. You can find their number in the phone book."

Rabbi Green stretched out his hand to me. While I held it, he wished me good luck in my search and I wished him good health. I leaned over to kiss his bald forehead. The leaves on the magnolia trees outside waved in the spring breeze.

Chapter Thirteen: Climb Ev'ry Mountain

Eager to call Deutsch for more details about the cremation—maybe Joey's ashes sat on a shelf in some warehouse in Cleveland and I could go fetch them today—I ran to the elevator down the hall and took it to the entrance floor of Mount Sinai. Patients young and old, Black and White, were roaming around in their green pajamas, buying coffee or a newspaper, some in wheelchairs, some on crutches, and others attached to IV drips on wheels. Visitors walked in carrying potted african violets wrapped in cellophane, or bouquets of flowers, concern coloring their faces. Others were walking out empty handed, some with satisfaction, as if joyful from the birth of a newborn, and some with fear and sadness in their eyes. At the candy and newspaper stand, a little boy was crying to his parents for a Baby Ruth. I asked the salesclerk to point me in the direction of the public phones.

As I walked toward a row of phones behind a low wall, men in green uniforms rushed past me, pushing an iron bed into an elevator. The fluorescent lighting and lack of windows made time disappear. Everyone moved within the eternal present of hospital time. As the orderlies disappeared with the bed into someone else's sorrow, I slid into a phone booth and looked in all directions. Isn't that what Joe Friday did on *Dragnet* when he wanted to make an important call?

I closed the door, looked up Sid Deutsch in the white pages, and dialed. A woman's voice answered, offering a tentative "Hello," as though she were a visitor in a house of mourning.

"I'd like to talk to Sid Deutsch," I countered at full volume. Never had I felt so determined.

"Regarding what matter?" she asked, her tone pleasant and caring.

"It's about my baby brother, Joey, who was cremated in 1951."

"I'll put you right through," she said.

Her rapid and positive response caught me off guard. No sooner had I taken a deep breath than a cheerful

"Hellooo," with an inappropriate, extended *o* that turned into a *u*, as if the speaker had just won a lottery, came through the receiver. "Sid Deutsch here."

"Hello," I said, uncharacteristically assertive. My Israeli persona had no patience for American pleasantries. "I'm calling to get some information about a cremation you did of my brother in 1951 at the request of the Billow's company in Akron." Listening to my own words, I couldn't believe I was really doing this, playing detective. How long would it take for the rest of me to catch up to this confident, assertive voice?

"Sure," he said. "I remember those folks. Used to go down there whenever Mr. Billow called because a Jewish baby had died. Sometimes they'd bring the body up to Cleveland, or they'd send it to Fort Wayne if I wasn't available." He hesitated and then continued. "If I'm not mistaken, there's a shopping center there now."

I had no interest in the historical geography of Akron, Ohio. Jerusalem provided me with enough of that. I wanted facts, just the facts, and here was this man, Deutsch, trying to divert me with urban renewal.

"I don't give a damn about any fucking shopping center," I said, surprising not only him but myself as well. "Do you know where my brother's ashes are?"

"Gee, ma'am," he stammered. "I understand this is still pretty raw with you, but I can't talk to someone who uses language like that." During the lingering silence, as my pulse went down, I felt remorse. But it was too late. "I'm afraid I can't help you," he said. "Have a real good day now."

The fucking bastard hung up on me, taking my swearing personally rather than as an expression of my belated unresolved grief. I needed help and understanding, not lessons in manners. Grateful I had so many quarters in my wallet, I calmed down enough to dial a long-distance operator, got the number of Billow's in Akron, and reached them on the first try. An instrumental version of "Climb Ev'ry Mountain" played over the line until the sleepy voice of a woman who sounded like she had witnessed too many deaths for one lifetime said, "Good afternoon. Billow's Funeral Homes and Crematory. How can I help you?"

"I'm trying to gather information about my baby brother, Joey, who died in 1951," I said.

I didn't need to say anything more because she replied immediately. "Hold on, please. I'll have a look in our files. What did you say the name was?"

"I didn't. It's George Joseph Stonehill."

She put me on hold. More *Sound of Music*. *Ford ev'ry stream* . . . This was happening too fast. Now I wanted some of that historical geography to slow down the process. Listening to "Climb Ev'ry Mountain" made me miss my children, who had watched *The Sound of Music* a thousand times. Would they think their mother was crazy if they knew what she was doing?

There was no running away from the past. I was sure Maria von Trapp, after settling in Vermont, suffered from homesickness for the specific hills that were alive with her primary music. The woman's voice interrupted the recording right before *till you find your dream*. "Sorry to keep you waiting," she said, sounding more awake now. "I have here in my hands a file on your brother, and it has two documents. Would you like me to make copies and put them in the mail to you?"

I was speechless.

"I'm sorry. Can you hear me? I said I can send you copies. Two pieces of paper."

This was so easy. Why had it taken me so long to act? "Yes. Yes, of course. That would be most kind. Thank you so much."

Assertion got results. Maybe I would adapt that stance in my family life as well, learn how to tell Elliot what I needed. "You have no idea how much this means to me."

At the same time, much to my shock, an unfamiliar anger rumbled inside. How dare this Akron Julie Andrews confine my brother to two stinking documents? He was almost two when he died, part of a family, certainly worth more than two sheets of paper.

I gave the woman in Akron my address in Israel, and after she refused my offer to pay the postage and oohed and aahed about my living in the real, earthly Jerusalem and told me how she had always wanted to visit the Holy Land with First Methodist but her husband was scared and never let her go and now it was too late, we said goodbye and hung up.

I stood in the phone booth another five minutes, forcing myself to breathe normally. What time zone was I in? Past or present? And where? Mount Sinai? Mount Zion?

* * *

Despite my apparent success uncovering reliable facts about Joey's death, something within me still needed Joey alive. There was no other explanation for the burst of imagination that followed.

Chapter Fourteen: The Outrageous Fiction, Lillian, Continued

The staff at Woody Haven was devastated when Lillian went to her final resting place so unexpectedly in 1973. Their sadness was nothing compared to Joey's. On the morning she died, he had hugged her dead body all day, waiting for the words from his favorite song, "Go Down Moses," and those verses from Isaiah that he loved. "Wake up, Lillian," he screamed, again and again. "We gotta go to work." Lillian didn't budge. He lay next to her all morning and afternoon, hungry and thirsty, until four thirty, when the phone rang. Joey rolled over Lillian's body, and by the eighth ring he had reached the phone. It was the night nurse from Woody Haven.

"Why ain't you and Lillian here, Joey? It's almost five o'clock."

"She's sleeping," Joey cried.

Within fifteen minutes, Horace, a male nurse from Woody Haven, pushed open the back porch door, entered the bungalow, and saw the scene for himself. He leaned over Lillian's face and held her wrist. He helped Joey sit up. "Let's get you dressed, pal. We gotta go to work." Joey heard Horace cover Lillian with their sheet. "I'm afraid she's gone."

"Gone where?" Joey said, angry at Horace. Who did he think he was, barging into their home like this?

"She's solid gone, Joey. Passed on . . . gone home . . . called back." Horace spoke softly, and with reverence. This made it harder for Joey to hear and understand. All those words. What was he saying? He knew his opposites. The opposite of solid was liquid. What was Horace talking about? *This* was Lillian's home.

"She's tired," Joey said. "You'll see. Soon she'll wake up and drink her coffee, no milk, two sugars. You better take the sheet off her." He put his hand on the sheet over what he thought was Lillian's head. Then he put his hand on his forehead and prayed.

"Come on, Joey," Horace said, lifting him into a standing position. "We gotta get you dressed and get outta here and go to work."

"But I ain't never been to work without Lillian." Joey tried to sit down on the bed, but Horace held him upright.

"So this is the first day," Horace said, easing Joey onto the only chair in the room. He took Joey's clothes off the hooks on the back of the bedroom door, dressed him, and led him toward the bedroom door.

Joey stopped and turned back toward the bed. "Don't leave me, Lillian. Don't die. Not today. Not ever." He coughed and choked. Tears formed in the corner of his eyes, and he wiped them away with the back of his hand.

"That's okay, fella," Horace said. "You should cry after all Lillian's done for you. Cry for me too, pal. We all loved Lillian. God is taking good care of her now. You can be sure of that, Joey. He owes her. He owes her big time."

Horace walked Joey over to his crutches, which were leaning against the wall. Even though Joey was twenty-four, he barely had the weight of a fifteen-year-old. When he collapsed into a boneless heap on the floor, Horace picked him up gently and carried him out of the bungalow over his left shoulder. Joey's legs flailed, and he pounded Horace's back with both hands. While pounding, he bawled, "Why did she leave me? Why did she die? She promised to stay with me forever."

Horace and Joey sat in the front seat of the Billow's Chevy, both crying.

From that afternoon, Joey lived in a room on the first floor of Woody Haven. Dr. Small arranged it; he had grown fond of the boy and knew he was responsible for his welfare. He had also loved Lillian. She had taught him, as well as the whole staff, something invaluable about the power of love. "You stay here as long as you want," Small told Joey.

Joey spent his afternoons and nights sitting next to the women who operated the switchboard—Nancy in the afternoon and Carol at night. He was used to sleeping from early morning until noon. After a few weeks he wanted to learn how to operate "the phones," as Nancy called them, but Carol said a blind kid with CP could never operate what she called "the system."

"I can say the Pledge of Allegiance and hold my hand on my heart," Joey said.

"That's not going to help you answer phones, Joey."

"I know the first chapter of Genesis by heart," he said.

Joey's words touched Carol. Poor kid, deserted by his own family as a baby, and then the only person in the world who cared for him, a woman holy as a saint, full of love and devotion, upped and died. Carol felt sorry for him, but she wasn't about to teach him how to operate a switchboard. What she did do was give him a radio. All during the night shift, while he sat next to her, he listened to the radio at full volume. That is how, on the evening of October 6, 1973, Joey learned that Israel had been attacked by the Egyptian and Syrian armies. Carol was talking on the phone to her mother in Toledo.

"Did you hear that?" he shouted at Carol.

"Hear what? I'm talking to my mom."

"The news," Joey said, and gave her the transistor. "The Hebrews have been attacked." He couldn't prevent his lower legs from spasming, and they kicked Carol's chair. His arms flailed all over the telephone corner.

"Calm down, Joey. It's far away," Carol said, and then, "Goodbye," to her mom.

"But I'm a Hebrew," Joey said, as if on fire. "Lillian told me."

"We're all God's children," Carol said.

He took his crutches and started walking toward the front door of Woody Haven.

"Where do you think you're going, Mr. Joey?" Carol stood right behind him.

"I have to help save the Hebrews from Amalek. Lillian said if I ever can help one Hebrew, it is my duty to do so." He walked into the wall and fell to the floor. He turned his face toward Carol, who was standing above him. His face contorted with emotion. "Help me, Carol! I must save the Children of Israel."

Carol bent down and put her hand on his head. "Relax, Joey. The Children of Israel will do just fine without you." She led him back to his room, gave him a sleeping pill, and told him to get a good night's rest.

All during the war that the radio called the Yom Kippur War, Joey was glued to his transistor. He couldn't sleep, even with pills. Dr. Small didn't know how to calm him down. Only Lillian had been able to calm Joey.

The staff at Woody Haven held a meeting and decided to humor Joey. "Okay," Dr. Small told him on the tenth day of the war, when it looked like Israel might crumble, "you can go over there. Go save the Hebrews, Joey. Go help the Children of Israel."

Joey would have jumped if he could. Instead, a smile bridged his shining face from ear to ear. "Lillian said I should," he repeated, over and over again, until finally the whole staff at Woody Haven began to believe that Joey, a twenty-four-year-old blind Hebrew who suffered from cerebral palsy, might save the Israeli nation. Crazier things than this had come out of that land.

* * *

"Don't call me crippled," Joey yelled at the agent at Cleveland Hopkins International Airport when he overheard him ask for a wheelchair "for a young crippled guy." It was October 27 and Joey was on his way to JFK Airport. From there he would take a direct flight to Israel, a gift from the staff at Woody Haven. Some people from ALYN Hospital in Jerusalem had promised Dr. Small they would meet Joey at the airport. He would stay at the hospital and fill in, as much as he could, for employees who had been called up to fight.

"Don't call me crippled, sir," he repeated to the airline agent in New York, who didn't even have the decency to talk in his direction. "Call me physically challenged," he said with great effort, as he slipped his ticket into his coat pocket. "Or, better yet, call me Joey."

Chapter Fifteen: Ms. Page

By the time I returned to my home in Jerusalem from Cleveland, the envelope from Billow's Funeral Homes and Crematory was waiting for me.

In addition to another copy of Joey's Certificate of Death (document 1), the envelope contained a form for ACCT. # 30133 (document 2). My reading of #30133 told me that Billow's Funeral Homes and Crematory received "BABY STONEHILL" from Woody Haven. Apparently only later was Billow's informed that "Baby 30133" had a name. George Joseph was "taken to Deutsch Funeral Home, Cleveland"—that is, somebody must have driven him, but the name of the driver was indecipherable.

The form is a funeral home intake record reading, in part:

NAME ~~GEORGE JOSEPH~~ ~~BABY~~ STONEHILL — DATE OF INTERMENT FEB 24 1951 — ACCT No. 30133

ADDRESS 2849 LUDLOW RD SHAKER HEIGHTS 20 CLEVELAND, OHIO

SERVICES AT NONE — DAY — HOUR

REV.

BURIAL — (SEC.) CEMETERY — BOX VAULT

SHIP Sent to Deutsch Funeral Home, Cleveland — DEVICE-TRIM TENT

STAFF DIRECTOR — PAPERS NO

HEARSE — DATE OF DEATH FEB. 24, 1951 — AGE 2 YRS

CHAIRS — TELEPHONE LONGACRE 1-9054 (CLEVELAND) RESIDENCE PROSPECT 1-5360-805.

FLOWERS — SURVIVORS NEIL + RITA STONEHILL PARENTS

SEDAN

ORGANIST

30133

FLOWER DISPOSITION

HOW MANY PAMPHLETS

AUTO LIST

JEWELRY

DELIVER CASKET — DAY — HOUR

TO — FRIENDS MAY CALL AT

EMBALMER no

DOOR BADGE — CHURCH LODGES

TRAFFIC ESCORT — WHERE EMPLOYED

DIED AT WOODY HAVEN — VETERAN? WHICH WAR BURIAL FLAG?

WILL SELECT — LENGTH OF ILLNESS HAIR

AUTOPSY — NAIL POLISH? CLOTHING

AMB. ACCT.

According to the form, there were no announcements of Joey's death in any papers. There was no need for a hearse or chairs, mourners, flowers, sedan, or organist. There was no service, no burial, no pamphlets, no autos to list or jewelry to adorn the dead. There was no embalmer, no door badges, and no traffic escort. There was no autopsy, and seemingly, no illness, as the line for "length of illness" was empty. On the body of Joey, who was not a United States veteran, there was no nail polish or clothing. Friends could not call.

Official bureaucratic forms can lie. One cannot rely on them for historical truth. This form stated that the only survivors were "Parents: Neil and Rita." The absence of two other survivors—Elizabeth and me—screamed from the earth. Number 30133 erased me from my personal history.

I mulled over this official document for months until the assertive stranger who had expressed herself in the Cleveland phone booth felt comfortable in my Jerusalem skin. How could I convince Miriam to deliver a bat mitzvah speech in front of a crowd if her own mother could not stand up to a form? I would not take Billow's historical affronts to truth without responding!

My first preference was to contact Woody Haven Boarding Home, because they had supplied Billow's with the information, but the telephone operator in Cleveland had told me in 1988 that no such place was listed in the Akron phone book. Apparently, Woody Haven had gone out of business. Or had been driven out of business? I wasn't about to leave Jerusalem for Akron to investigate the matter. Besides, by 1990 I had gathered enough facts—both reliable and un—that they were beginning to take second place to my primary need: the expression of frustration and anger at the whole Joey conundrum.

I didn't require a real person for this.

Ms. Lynda Page, Director
Woody Haven Boarding Home
18 West 49th Street
Akron, OH

Dear Ms. Page,

It may seem strange receiving a letter in 1990 from earthly Jerusalem asking about something that happened in 1951 in Akron, Ohio. Nonetheless, I hope you will be able to guide me to the land of personal truth. I am the mother of three wonderful healthy children, but periodically I can't get out of bed in the morning due to my unresolved grief at the death of my baby brother Joey on February 24, 1951.

I'm writing you because of a form I received from Billow's Funeral Homes and Crematory (ACCT. #30133). On this form it states that the only survivors of Joey's death were my parents. I can only assume that all the information on the form was supplied by someone at Woody Haven, where Joey was treated, supposedly, for pneumonia, from January 20–February 24, 1951, as per his Certificate of Death.

This oversight on the survivors list erases me from my history.

Do sisters have no status in Akron?

Being a reasonable person, I know the form sent from Billow's for ACCT. #30133 is only a document, but a document is a text and since we live through our texts, this specific one *must* be amended. I will not be erased from my past. Not by you or any other Akronian asshole. The information regarding survivors is historically incomplete. Somebody in Akron made Elizabeth and me invisible, took us out of the rubric and thereby out of the scene. Our names do not appear.

Please correct this distortion of history by adding our names to the list of survivors. Also, note that my father's name is N*ea*l, not N*ei*l.

I may have been short for my age in 1951, and too quiet because my thumb plugged my mouth, and I may have hummed instead of talked, but I assure you, Ms. Page, today I am making my mark on the world.

Finally, I would appreciate some reliable information. Maybe a Gwyneth or a Lillian who lives down the block in Akron remembers who called my parents on a

Sunday night in February 1951 to tell them Joey died. What time was the call made? How much snow fell that day? The more specific the details, the faster will be my recovery from this prolonged, obsessive, and delayed mourning. A story with a beginning, middle, and end will help me "move on," as you say in America. If you can't provide this information, I will have to make it up. In order to let go of the past, Ms. Page, I need one.

Enclosed please find an SASE for your reply.

Sincerely,

J. L.

Encl.

Chapter Sixteen: Dear Joey

February 24, 1992

Dear Joey,

It never occurred to me to write you until now. I'm writing today because Michael, your oldest nephew, is leaving home in three days. He's going into the army. No amount of preparation enables me to survive this trauma—my firstborn leaving home. And I have been preparing myself from the day he first lifted his head in the playpen at three months old.

I hate saying goodbye to those I love, Joey. I fear they will die or I will die or someone in the family will die. Love, leaving, and death are all mixed up. If I love someone too much, that person will die.

It's strange how you came into my life again when Joseph, my third and youngest, was hospitalized with convulsions. I thought he would die like you did. Since that time I have learned to appreciate the differences and variations among separation, abandonment, and simply saying goodbye. Someone says goodbye, leaves, and comes back: separation. Someone doesn't say goodbye, leaves, and doesn't come back: abandonment. Someone doesn't say goodbye, leaves, and comes back: confusing.

Joey, I felt abandoned when you disappeared. Nobody said, "He's not coming back." Nobody told me where I could find you. Maybe *you* floated up to the castle's high ceiling and were sucked through the secret hole and released into space. I stayed home, wondering.

Later I needed to be left, abandoned, and rejected again and again. Or ignored and erased over and over. With practice I imagined one could master abandonment. Fortunately, only part of me became invisible. There was another part always watching to see how these duets played out.

It occurs to me now, as I write you, that maybe you were not the only person in the family who abandoned me at midcentury. Why else would the obsession remain after I have all the facts? I'm focused on you, my phantom brother, here and not here. But Mom and Dad abandoned me as well, certainly emotionally, at least on that fateful day when the rabbi came and told us you died.

Some people here on earth believe spoken words can save us, but back in 1951 I didn't have words, nor did anyone else in the family. *Shut down* was the clear message emanating from our parents. Rabbi Green offered some words, thank God. I started learning written words in first grade, their spelling, pronunciation, their positions on the lines. (Always the line, *don't get outta line*.) But all the infinite combinations of words were insufficient to understand your death. Only after I became a mother of three did I start diving into *myself* for the words—those black stones buried in tar, covered by decades of coal silence. I dredged them one by one from the cave of remembrance, next to the cave of imagination.

Where are you, Joey? According to my calculations you would now be forty-three years old. (Does anyone count where you are, or is it always forever?)

With no gravestone, you had no boundaries, no lines between the living and dead. I breathed on earth, but you lay dead inside me, so part of me was dead. Though you were dead, you lived inside me, so part of you was alive. Even as I write this in simple English, I am baffled by the paradox. Life within death. Death within life. After you left, Mom was never the same. There was an emptiness inside her. No matter how good I was or how smart Elizabeth or how cute Jimmy, the brother who came after you, nothing filled the hollowness for years. She housed a dark cave, an abyss where one name dangled from an umbilical cord.

These are nouns I use to revivify you: spirit, imp, sprite, specter, ghost, shade, shadow, phantom. But nouns are not enough, nor are still lives, fantasies, fictions, facts, memories, documents, or letters.

I need a story, Joey. I need embodied details, facts lived through family, to anchor me to our past.

I've started to write one. It's called "Mount Zion, A Chronicle."

Sending love and a gentle hug,

Your sister,

Judy

Part Two: Mount Zion, A Chronicle

But upon Mount Zion there shall be deliverance…

Obadiah 1:17

Neal suspected Freund, the Babe Ruth of obstetricians, was hiding something. Rita had been in there eight hours, and nobody was telling him anything. What could he do? Freund was no trucker. Neal knew how to talk to truckers, but a doctor? Cleveland's best? Neal was paying him a fortune to deliver what he hoped would be their first boy. How could he tell Freund to go to hell?

At five Freund had deigned to nod from the top of his highfalutin white coat, but nothing since then. If they ever had a fourth, it wouldn't be at Mount Zion.

Magnolias along East Boulevard fluttered beyond the waiting room window. A perfect evening for baseball. He had finished all the daily papers. The Indians made him sick, what with Bob Lemon unable to hit with any consistency and Rosen, the Jew, striking out at the bottom of the ninth with Feller on third. Made his blood boil. The front page was no better. How much Truman could he take? Harry "Ass" Truman. Should never have stopped selling hats in Missouri.

Alone in the waiting room, Neal lifted his fedora from the seat next to him and placed it on his bald head, making sure the crease was exactly in the center. He slipped on his jacket—"Take the rain one," Rita had said on their way out—and tapped out a Camel from the half-empty pack in the jacket's right-hand pocket.

"Long day for you, gramps?" This from a new guy, walking in to take a seat. In a black-and-red work shirt, he looked like some teenage logger from southern Ohio.

"No," Neal said, feeling around for the lighter in the other pocket. "It's my missus." He sensed the man doing the arithmetic behind his broad forehead. They all reacted this way when he told them. *Yeah, that's right, bud,* he felt like saying, *I'm the father, and in one of those rooms my beautiful twenty-eight-year-old Rita is finally giving me a son, I hope, so shut up and mind your own goddamned business.* But he only talked that way to truckers.

"Your first?" Neal said as he lit the Camel.

"Second," the boy said. "First was a boy last year."

Neal was old enough to be this guy's father. He was angry at the young punk for making him feel like a fool.

"Bye now, Mr. Stonehill. You be good now," a nurse walked by and called out, all smiles. "We're takin' good care of the missus."

They were all making fun of him, talking about him behind his back. Neal tipped his hat to her as he walked to the elevator, and stubbed out his Camel after two puffs.

The ground floor was quieter now than when they had arrived that morning. He breezed through the open door, rather than use the revolving one. Revolving doors made him dizzy.

The air in the parking lot was thick as egg whites. No surprise there. It had been wet and muggy for days, though a little rain never stopped the Indians. Actually, maybe the weather *was* causing them to play so lousy. He took out his keys and opened the Chrysler. A thin film of damp dust covered the yellow paint. The car looked gray. Maybe he'd take it to Harvey's for a good cleaning, inside and out, "the woiks," as Harvey said. Yes, he would do that, before driving Rita and the baby home. How long would they have to stay here? Probably a week, like with the girls. Yes, he would clean the car. But this one was early, not like the girls. She always liked the car when it was clean and didn't smell from Camels. "Can't you change brands," she'd say every time she settled into the passenger seat. "I read Viceroy doesn't smell. It has a cork top or tip, whatever you call it." His little Rita was so cute. Didn't know the first thing about cigarettes. He'd buy one of those smelly dangling things too, that made you think a pine forest was growing out of the windshield. That would make Reet happy.

Sitting in the driver's seat, he rested his forehead on the steering wheel and closed his eyes. Nerves. Sitting all day, pacing, reading, watching, making small talk, worried sick. He shook his head to get out of himself. He put the key in the ignition, turned it, and pressed the radio button. As soon as he heard "President Truman," he turned it off. Neal left the parking lot and took East 105th over to Chester, and from there drove to the parking lot in front of Howard Johnson's at University Circle. Lots of preemies did just fine. Only last week, when he was in Iowa, he had read in the *Gazette* about some twins born at the bottom of the seventh. Both were alive, in incubators. If some small-town doctor in Dubuque could succeed, there was no reason to doubt the skill of the great Dr. Manfred Freund of Cleveland, Ohio, operating out of Mount Zion, the best hospital in the Best Location in the Nation.

Even when a game was rained out in the eighth, there was a winner.

Neal parked near the exit sign, got out, took off his jacket, and walked toward the orange roof. What were the girls' favorite flavors? Fudge ripple? Chocolate mint chip? Hell, he thought, all twenty-eight were delicious. The familiar smells of greasy hamburgers and french fries, bacon, and apple pie conjured up a smorgasbord in the thick air. Sure beat the smell of ammonia over at Mount Zion.

"One?" the receptionist asked, and after he nodded and removed his hat, she motioned him to the back of the restaurant. There another hostess pointed him to a booth. He slid onto the vinyl seat, took out a cigarette, and slid the ashtray toward him from below the jukebox. He lit a Camel and inhaled deeply, trying to relax. Christ, this was the damndest thing. Rita in the hospital all day and nothing to show for it. The girls took no time coming into the world. Maybe six hours, max. Boys were more stubborn, Ma had told him. He wished he could talk to his ma about that, but he didn't want to call her yet. She'd worry.

A waitress in a black uniform with a little white apron that covered her chest and stomach came over and gave him a glass of ice water and a menu.

What a day, with the water leaking out at eight thirty, while they were having their coffee and toast. She had stood up to give him a refill and whoosh, female liquid flooding the kitchen floor. He'd never seen anything like it and didn't know where she kept the mop.

"It's a sign," Rita moaned.

"What kind of sign?" He wanted more coffee.

"Dr. Freund said it was a sign to go to the hospital."

She held her belly from below as if the little thing might fall out right there on the kitchen floor. Neal called the doctor's office because she was scared. Some nurse or secretary said the doctor would meet them at Mount Zion in an hour. Dr. Freund was on an emergency call in the ghetto.

Neal had packed her suitcase. By the time they were ready to leave the house, Reet looked pale as butter. Neal called Vashti to come over right away to stay with the girls. Yes, he knew it was Saturday, and yes, she didn't work

Saturdays, but the missus had to get to the hospital pronto.

In thirty minutes she was there, her starched white apron covering the lap of her gray uniform, a fake ivory cigarette holder balanced on her lower lip. By then Rita was complaining of pains in her abdomen and short bouts of dizziness. Thank God the girls had stayed glued to the television set during the commotion. What a blessing that thingamajig was. A lifesaver, that TV set.

Now, alone in the restaurant booth after eight hours of waiting for new life at Mount Zion, Neal rested his cigarette in the ashtray, took a sip of ice water, and looked for a song on the jukebox. It was a tough choice. There was "Don't Cry, Joe," a slow number by some new guy named Frank Sinatra. Neal couldn't figure out what the big fuss was about Sinatra. Anyway, Neal needed something upbeat. He chose one of Reet's favorites, a song she'd sing in the kitchen on Sunday mornings while making the family their french toast. "A, You're Adorable—The Alphabet Song."

His mind started roving by *D*. Her contractions in the car, his pulling over to stop, her moaning, his not knowing which entrance of Mount Zion to use, their walking to the information desk, she holding her belly, he being told to rush her to emergency.

The waitress came and stood at the booth and tapped her fingers on the table to the music, question marks plastered all over her face. "Nice song," she said.

"Gimme a BLT on white toast," he said, pushing the menu toward her, "long on the mayonnaise."

"Anything else, sir?"

I, you're the one I idolize. Yes, that was how he felt about Rita.

"Anything else with that BLT?"

"Yeah. Make it to go," he said, standing up. He wanted to see her, rub those soft hands with their perfectly polished nails. He wanted to say something nice—*you make my life complete . . . you're awfully sweet . . .* how lucky he was to be married to the most beautiful woman in Cleveland. What a gift she had given him when she, a twenty-year-old beauty, agreed to marry him, a lonely, shy bachelor of thirty-eight from Fort Dodge, Iowa. How graceful she was when he first saw her skating at the Elysium Club the first month he had come to town. He wanted to thank her for making him a father, twice, and at his age. He knew he wasn't the best, not helping her enough with the girls, but maybe with a son things would be different. He'd take the little fella to ball games, teach him how to hold a bat and later a nine iron, read the financial page. He'd make Rita proud.

Now he would take the BLT back to Mount Zion, force Freund and the nurses to let him see his wife and his son, who, maybe, was being born this very minute. Christ, what was he doing in HoJo's?

U made my life complete.

He positioned his hat on his head. The waitress came over.

"Sir, is something the matter?"

The question gave Neal a start. "My wife's having a baby." This was the first time he said the words. He felt his spine stretch, his chin lift.

"Oh, we get a lot of those in here," she said. "Up at Mount Zion?"

He nodded.

"Well, you can relax, honey," she said. "They got real good doctors over there. It's a Jewish place, you know. I gotta cousin who's a nurse there."

He took a dollar fifty from his wallet and put it on the table for the BLT, but didn't wait for the sandwich.

Outside a gentle rain was falling, a June drizzle to welcome the new baby, cleanse Neal's worry and Rita's pain. He approached the Chrysler, singing, "U made my life complete," over and over until a tear fell on his upper lip. Or was it a rain drop? He wasn't sure.

* * *

Some quote held up the perimeter of the rotunda, but Neal couldn't make it out from the phone booth. Opposite him a woman in hospital pajamas leaned against the wall of another closed booth. She was crying and wiping her nose with her sleeve. Above the information desk hung a sign: "The Lord loves the Gates of Zion, Ps 87:2." What was that "Ps" about? Some afterthought? Obviously, the Lord had never spent eight hours in the waiting room.

"Stonehill residence," Vashti said, as she had been taught.

Her gruff smoker's voice forced Neal to focus. "It's me, Vashti. Mr. Stonehill."

"Sure is good to hear from you, Mister Neal. Is there a baby? We been waiting here all day watching the TV, eating lunch and dinner, getting all excited and wondering what's happening over there on Mount Zion."

Neal looked up at the perimeter again and bent his neck to see better. "Deliver," he made out. "No, Vashti, no baby yet." Christ, he should have called five hours ago. What was he thinking, that she would stay all day?

"Vashti, I wonder if you could sleep over tonight. The way things are going down here, I might not get back before midnight." He looked at his watch. "You can use the room upstairs."

"Sure, Mister Stonehill. I'll call Jephthah and let him know."

Neal wondered if Jephthah would visit while she was there and when exactly he'd manage to steal more scotch. Cowboy music from the TV blared in the living room. Vashti was asking him to give the missus a hug from her.

"I'll do that, Vashti. Now tell me, how were the girls?"

Elizabeth was finally looking at a book with a flashlight under her covers and the little one was still up, sucking her thumb, lying on the floor in front of the television. "Miracle it don't fall off," Vashti said. "That girl sure have one strong thumb."

Neal asked Vashti to put Elizabeth on the line. He heard her yell, "Come talk to your daddy, Lizzie," and cowboy music in the background.

He looked at his watch. Thirty-five minutes had passed since he'd left the waiting room. He turned his neck further this time and saw the whole word: "deliverance."

"Hi, Daddy. Where are you?"

"I'm at the hospital with your mom, Lizzie." When she didn't reply, he said, "Mount Zion, near Howard Johnson's."

"Oh." She breathed into the receiver and said nothing. Then, "Do I have a brother?"

"Not yet, sweetie." He tried not to sound worried.

"Judy says she wants a story, Daddy. Do I have to tell her one?"

Neal wanted to hang up and run upstairs. He bent down and turned further: ". . . there shall be deliverance . . ."

"I don't have any stories," he said. "Tell her that." Girls. They made you say the strangest things.

"Should I tell her to stop sucking her thumb, Daddy? Vashti says it will fall off by the time she's in first grade and then she won't be able to hold a pencil. When are you coming home?"

"Soon, Lizzie."

"I want a brother, Daddy."

"Me too, sweetie. Now give Vashti the phone."

Again the cowboy music. He imagined Roy Rogers riding Trigger over a desolate landscape, out there in Southern California, the palomino's legs slowing down only when they reached the Double R Bar Ranch. He pictured Roy spotting his wife from a distance. Dale Evans, queen of the West. She would be standing on the porch, pregnant, a smile on her face, wide as the country Roy had just crossed to reach her. Neal was humming "Happy Trails" by the time Vashti got back on the line.

"Yessir, Mister Stonehill. I'm right here."

"I'll pay you overtime, of course," Neal said, taking his wallet from his back pocket and checking he'd have enough to cover Vashti's pay.

"Don't you worry 'bout that, Mister Neal. Just pray that the missus be alright."

Upstairs, in the waiting room, a middle-aged guy had taken Neal's seat, but he found another empty one. The guy in his seat was flipping through the pages of *National Geographic*, a special issue on extinct species in North America. Neal had read it around noon. The man was showing drawings of weird creatures to an older gentleman sitting across the table from him, probably his father or father-in-law. They were laughing. Neal wished his own father had stuck around long enough to greet a first grandson. Missed it by a year, but the little boy—it had to be a boy!—would carry his name. Not the Steinberg, of course, which Neal had changed to Stonehill in '28 when he couldn't find work, but the Joseph. That, and Reet's father's name, George. If it was a boy, they had agreed during the top of the sixth, they would call him George Joseph Stonehill.

Neal stood up. He wanted to catch Freund as soon as he walked by. It didn't take long. Within minutes of his return, Neal saw the doctor, decked out in his pure white coat. Neal moved quickly to stand in front of him.

"Why hello there, Dr. Freund. Neal. Neal Stonehill. Perhaps I should call you Herr Doktor?" He extended his right hand in a way that Freund could not avoid.

"Yes, I know who you are, Neal," the doctor said. He extended his right hand, looking at the watch on his left wrist. "I'm sorry, I can't talk to you now," he said, letting go of his hand and walking toward the door that said Staff Only.

"I'm afraid that's not good enough, Doc," Neal said, following him. "I've been waiting in this hole of a waiting room all day for some news, a report, anything about Rita, and nobody's talking to me." He stepped closer to Freund's face. Three black hairs stuck out of his left nostril. Red lines, like streaks in strawberry ripple, crisscrossed the man's eyes. Neal made a fist with his right hand and raised it to his own chest.

Freund stepped back. "Hey, Neal. Get hold of yourself! Where do you think you are? This is a hospital, not a boxing ring."

Neal lowered his hand; his anger rose. "I know goddamned well where I am, Doc. I've been here all day and I want some answers. I want to see my wife and baby."

Freund looked into Neal's eyes. Neal couldn't tell whether there was pity or something else in that look, but it made him uneasy. He was certain: the whole crew was hiding something.

"What is it, Doc?" He put his fist in his pocket.

"I have a woman in the delivery room right now, Neal. Why don't you go home and we'll talk tomorrow."

Tomorrow? He wanted answers now. "I'm paying you, Freund," he said, looking straight into the doctor's eyes. He wondered why a man would go into such a business. Neal traveled the country. He saw the small towns of Indiana, Illinois, Minnesota, Iowa when he was on the road, towns peopled by the salt of the earth. He crossed the mighty Mississippi and heard the whispers of smaller tributaries. Like the back of his hand he knew Dubuque, Terre Haute, Toledo. He could tell when corn was ripe by its smell. Why would a man become an obstetrician? What did Freund see every day but dark, damp innards of strange women? Why would a man prefer blood and female juices to amber waves of grain?

"Tomorrow's not a possibility, Doc," Neal continued, stepping back an inch. "I'll wait right here. I got all night. Right here in this waiting room."

He had waited thirty-eight years to get married, another two for Elizabeth, two more for the little one, and another four for this one. What was one more night? He turned around and walked over to one of the empty chairs. He felt the stares of the other men. Was he a hero or a moron? He couldn't tell until the one with the extinct species patted his shoulder. "Good show, mister. You showed him who's boss."

By ten the drizzle had turned into the predicted torrents. The elms and magnolias waving in the streetlights looked like they were arguing with the devil. Neal felt himself doze off. He was sitting on a tin can behind his father's store in Fort Dodge. Two drunkards had fallen out of the saloon next door and were taking swings at each other, one calling the other a kike. A hand on his shoulder shook him awake.

"Mr. Stonehill, Mr. Stonehill."

He opened his eyes. A mature nurse stood above him. The badge across her breast pocket read "Lenore."

"How's my wife?"

"She's resting now, Mr. Stonehill. Dr. Freund asked that you come see him."

Neal looked at his watch. It was one in the morning. "About time," he muttered, standing to stretch. His lower back hurt. He remembered some eighth grader calling him a kike when he started junior high school and not knowing what it meant. The same kid accused him of killing Christ, but his ma told him he wasn't guilty. Neal rubbed his eyes hard with both hands, as if trying to get rid of the past, and followed Lenore through the Staff Only door, down the quiet hallway.

She stopped at a glass door boasting a gold plaque: "Dr. Manfred Freund, Obstetrician-Gynecologist." She knocked once and opened the door.

Freund had dark circles under his eyes, and those circles had circles. Was this how soldiers looked after days of battle? Neal felt a tinge of guilt for adding to the doctor's load, especially at this late hour.

"Thanks for seeing me now," Neal said. "I can see you're tired."

Freund offered him a Pall Mall from a gold cigarette case and slid his gold lighter over to him on the desk. It stopped right in front of Neal. They both lit up.

"Neal," Freund said. They both took deep drags.

Neal wished the office had a window so he could focus on a scrap of night sky, a star, or some wet branch. Now that he was sitting opposite Freund, he needed the freedom of the outdoors. For what? Deliverance? He felt confused and surveyed the walls. Certificates in black frames, many in foreign languages, hung in rows. Neal realized he knew nothing about Dr. Freund, other than his reputation for being the best obstetrician in Cleveland and a so-so golfer. Maybe it wasn't just the innards of strange women he saw. This man ushered in life. He delivered babies. What had Neal ever done that could compare to that?

"Neal," Freund repeated.

By the way Freund said his name, Neal could tell the news was not good. Was it pity in his tone? Was Neal pitiful? Neal put down his cigarette in the ashtray near him and let it burn. The day had burned everything out of him. Exhausted, he was ready for the truth. The time for evasions and pussyfooting was over. The truth would make him free, just like it said over the entrance to the *Cleveland Plain Dealer* building. "The Truth Shall Make You Free." Was this a bullshit message, or the real thing, like "The Lord Loves the Gates of Zion." And ". . . there shall be deliverance . . ."

"You wouldn't believe the way those people live down there in the ghetto, Neal."

Freund was playing with a loose cuticle on his left thumb and seemed to want to talk about his emergency in the ghetto. Neal wasn't interested. Not now, not at one in the morning, after a whole day in the waiting room. All he cared about was Rita and their new baby. "How's Reet?" he said. Still, he wondered if Freund worked these hours all the time or if today had been an exception. Freund had kids, didn't he? Did he ever see them? He was a golfer. Neal knew he played at Oakwood, where the hoi polloi of German Jews mixed with each other. One day he and Rita would join a country club.

Freund stood up and left his cigarette to burn in his own ashtray. He walked toward the corner of the room. His white coat looked dirty and wrinkled. "There's no easy way to tell you this, Neal," he said, turning toward his degrees, touching one and then straightening another as if *they* were his children, then finally thrusting his jittery hands deep inside the pockets of his white coat. Neal imagined all the secrets doctors kept were buried in the folds of those pockets. Freund faced the wall, his back to Neal.

Neal considered jumping him from behind. He had seen that move in enough westerns. All he had to do was wind his arm around the doctor's neck and dig his thumb into the guy's back as if it were a gun. It always brought results. Freund was no cowboy. Neal could easily beat him up. He picked up his cigarette, drew a long swag, and listened to the man's low drone.

"You have a . . ."—Freund swallowed—"a son, Neal. You have a son." Now he turned around to face Neal.

Neal let out a loud *whew* with his next exhale and shook his head from side to side in disbelief, even though he couldn't imagine any other result. It had to be a son. Two girls were enough. He smiled as if the doctor had told him he had won a lottery. He considered standing up and shaking Freund's hand, but something in Freund's tone glued him to his seat.

"That's just wonderful, Dr. Freund," he said. "You know, I'm not a young man. Forty-six last January. I've been waiting for this day for years. I'm just sorry my own father isn't here to share the happiness. Thank you, Doc."

He was sorry he hadn't bought cigars, but there had been no time to prepare with the birth coming five weeks early and all hell breaking loose in the kitchen. Why hadn't he bought cigars at HoJo's? Why wasn't the doctor shaking *his* hand?

"You sure kept me waiting a long time. In '43 and '45 you almost came skipping into the waiting room to tell me the good news." Neal was sorry he said that. This was no time to accuse Freund of wrongdoing or neglect. "I'd like to see Rita, Doc."

Freund walked back to his chair and sat down. "Come back in the morning, Neal. I'll talk to you and Rita together then. I'll explain everything."

Explain? What was there to explain? Had Mount Zion changed its policies? Neal crushed his cigarette in the ashtray. "I want to see Rita and the baby now," he said.

"I'm afraid that's impossible, Neal. Nine thirty, ten in the morning. Then we'll sit in Rita's room and talk. It's been a long day." Freund rubbed the corner of his eye with one finger, stood up again, and walked to the door. He opened it and stood there in silence.

Neal felt like punching him, this time in the nose, but when Neal stood up, turned toward the door, and Freund extended his hand, Neal shook it and said, "Thanks, Doctor. I'll see you in the morning," and walked down the hall.

In the elevator new names rained from the walls. George and Joseph sounded too Old World, too part of the past. Maybe Bob, as in Bob Feller, or Al, for Al Rosen.

Neal offered a Camel to the uniformed elevator man working the night shift. "It's a boy," Neal said, a little embarrassed, and this embarrassment surprised him. Hadn't he always wanted a son? Hadn't he dreamt of this moment when he could hand out cigars?

The man smiled and put the cigarette in his shirt pocket. "First grandson?" he asked.

"First son," said Neal.

"Glory be," the man said. "Hey, pops, you take good care of him now."

Before he left the building, Neal lifted his jacket over his head. Rain was falling with no respite. He ran to the car, rain attacking from all directions. By the time he sat in the driver's seat, he was drenched.

Drenched and the father of a son, Neal turned the key in the ignition. When the little bugger turned two, he would buy him his first mitt; at three, a junior bat. By four they would go downtown Saturday afternoons on the rapid transit and walk over to Cleveland Stadium to watch the Indians clobber the Yanks. Neal would buy him a hot dog before the game and another during the seventh inning stretch, easy on the mustard. They would play catch in the driveway when Neal came home early from work. As soon as the little boy—maybe Early, for Early Wynn?—could hit and run, Neal would sign him up for Little League.

Finally, a son.

Going up Murray Hill, Neal turned on the radio. Ezio Pinza was singing "Some Enchanted Evening." *You may meet a stranger across a crowded room* . . . Wasn't that his story? Reet's soft brown wavy hair flying in the cold air behind her as she took the corners with ease, strength, and grace, skimming the ice like an angel so that his heart jumped when her right skate crossed her left on the turn. Yes, she would go out with him, she had replied when he'd dared to ask for a date while the ice was being cleaned. Yes, he would marry her, he'd told himself when they skated what would become their first couples' skate at the end of the evening. Yes, she would give him sons.

At the light on Fairhill, he remembered he hadn't kissed her goodbye when the nurse scooted her into emergency. Why hadn't anyone let him see her? Questions clawed and dampened his reverie.

At home Vashti dozed on the living room couch, the fanny spoon tucked under her pillow. She sat up when Neal walked into the room. "It's a boy," he whispered.

"Glory be," she said, rubbing her eyes. "Isn't that marvelous, Mister Stonehill." She covered her legs with the blanket from the upstairs room.

"I have to be down there at nine thirty in the morning," Neal said. "Can you stay until noon?"

Her lips pursed. He thought she was disappointed. "Sure thing, Mister Stonehill. I'll just call Jephthah and let him know."

"Don't tell the little ones," Neal said.

Vashti looked at him as if this were the craziest request in the world.

"I want to tell them myself," he added.

"Yessir," she said. "Do you want me to put those wet clothes in the dryer?"

Neal had forgotten his soaked clothes. He shook his head. "No need," he told her. "You go back to sleep now. I'll be out early in the morning."

He walked into his bedroom, shut the door, undressed, and hung the clothes in the bathroom. Dressed in his striped pajamas, he crawled into his side of the bed and lay on his back. How . . . enchanting . . . Yes, that was the word. All the tension and nerves of the day sank into the mattress. He rubbed his thighs and lower back, naming each uncomfortable chair in the waiting room. But the waiting had been worthwhile. Now he was the father of a son.

But why hadn't Freund told him more? The questions kept him awake. Weight, height, color of eyes and hair. Was he fair like the Russian side or dark like the Hungarians? Neal turned onto his side. In the morning he would make a list. Then he would call Ma and his sisters and brothers and Rita's mom and see if she could babysit.

Again, names popped into his head: Mickey (Vernon) Stonehill. Lou (Boudreau) Stonehill. He turned onto his other side and stretched his arm across to the empty pillow next to him. In a week Reet would be back in bed with him and their family would be complete. George Joseph, or whatever his name would be, would get the room across the hall. The two little girls would share the bedroom at the end of the hall next to the kitchen. He couldn't believe his good fortune. To think that a Jewish punk from Fort Dodge, son of poor Ukrainian immigrants, could make it so big.

He drifted into sleep, imagining Ezio Pinza and Mary Martin, their first kiss at night on a beach, under a date palm, the Pacific Ocean lulling them into dreamland.

* * *

In the morning Neal slipped out of the house before the girls awoke. He wouldn't call anyone just yet. He didn't want to be bombarded by questions he couldn't answer.

The rain had stopped, but the roads were still wet and the grass on the lawn in front of Mount Zion was waterlogged. Bad day for golf. He sat in the car to write his questions and then, with his list in his pocket, he walked briskly into the rotunda, pausing to read the headlines at the newsstand. Bill Veeck was considering selling the Cleveland Indians? How could the bastard do such a thing after they had won the pennant last year? So what if the potential buyers were former Clevelanders, Bob Hope among them? This Veeck had no civic pride. Neal bought the paper, stuffed it under his arm, and took the elevator up to the sixth floor, maternity.

Signs demanding silence dominated the gray walls. He walked to the nurses' station and asked a nurse named Beth for Rita's room number. A bizarre question mark sprouted on Beth's face. Had she never seen a man over forty visiting the maternity ward? Beth poked the nurse sitting next to her in the waist and, never taking her eyes off Neal, said, "This is Mr. Stonehill." They both stared as though he were on the wrong floor on the wrong day, even at the wrong hospital. He felt pitiful and was pissed. Instead of congratulating him, greeting him with sugar, they offered lemons.

"Mrs. Stonehill is in room six," Beth said, pointing to her left.

Neal walked down the quiet, empty hallway. The door was slightly ajar. He took a deep breath. Bases loaded, two outs and he's walking to the plate. He poked his head into the room. Rita was asleep under the green piqué hospital blanket. He walked in quietly and closed the door behind him. The room smelled of fresh ammonia. He walked to the window, opened it, and put his paper on the Formica chair between the bed and the window.

His princess lay on her back sleeping, wearing the pink nightgown he had packed. Was it only yesterday? Even after the long day of labor and birth, she was beautiful, though she looked pale. Had she lost blood during the birth? He sat down and inched the chair closer to the bed. Her breathing was quiet. He looked at his watch. Already nine fifteen. Freund would be in soon. He put a hand on her shoulder, bent over, and planted a kiss on her forehead. She twitched her head.

"Honey," he whispered, as if any more force might cause harm.

She opened her eyes for a second and then shut them. The skin on her eyelids was damp as the grass outside.

"You're tired, sweetheart," he said. "The doctor will be here soon to talk to us."

Her face lacked expression. Maybe she was drugged, still under the stuff from the mask. That must be it. He stood up and walked into the hallway. At the other end, Dr. Freund was talking to the two nurses at the station. Neal walked toward him.

"Morning, Dr. Freund," he said, feigning an upbeat attitude. Freund looked exhausted. "The missus is tired, but I'm sure I can wake her if you're ready for us now."

"I'll be right there, Neal," he said.

Freund always seemed to be showing him the way out.

Back in room six he was amazed to see Rita had pulled the blanket up to her nose. Her eyes were open, but she didn't focus on anything.

Neal rushed to her side and kissed her forehead again. "Good morning, sweetheart," he said, this time louder. She did not respond. "One for you," he said, and then kissed her again. "And one for the little fella." Still leaning over her face, he added, "You have made me very happy, sweetheart." While he was still close to Rita's face, the doctor walked in.

"Morning, Rita," Freund said

She did not respond. Neal straightened, turned to the doctor, and in a soft voice said, "What's wrong with her?"

"She had a hard day yesterday, Neal. It takes a while for the anesthetic to wear off. She lost a lot of blood. It was a difficult birth."

Freund walked to the chair on the other side of Rita's bed and sat down. "I was just talking to the nurses about the baby." He looked at them both.

"When can I see him, Doc?" Neal stood next to Rita, his hand on her head.

Freund took a deep breath, his eyes on the blanket covering Rita's mouth. "There's no easy way to tell you this, Neal. Rita isn't responding now, but I know she can hear me and understands everything I am saying."

Neal's fingers started to tingle and feel numb.

"There's no simple way to tell you this . . .," Freund repeated.

"Tell us what, Doc?" Neal needed a cigarette.

"Your baby, your son, that is . . ." He looked down at the floor and then at the light bulb dangling from the ceiling, as if searching for the right words. "He's a beautiful little thing."

Neal bent his fingers to get rid of the tingling. The baby probably had jaundice. Maybe he needed a few days in an incubator. After all, he was a preemie. No big deal. That's what happened in Dubuque. "Yes, well, he probably inherited those good looks from Rita," Neal said.

"Yes, his features are delicate and he's a beautiful baby, but . . ." Freund looked uneasy and squeamish, as if he had never sat with new parents before. It made Neal nervous.

"When can I see him?"

"The little fella has some problems."

Neal heard "fella" and thought of the great Bob Feller. Neal didn't understand what Freund meant by problems. He hated pussyfooting. He had waited long enough. Now he wanted numbers: height, weight, all those details doctors were so good at. He could deal with numbers. Hell, he could calculate in his head the time and distance between Fort Wayne and Toledo, Terre Haute and

Cleveland. He knew batting averages, runs batted in, and other statistics that made baseball so fascinating. He wanted to go out now and buy his son his first pack of baseball cards.

"It seems the baby didn't get enough oxygen at birth."

The first pitch, a strike. Neal repeated the words softly—*oxygen, birth*. He sort of knew what oxygen was, though he never took chemistry in high school, if they even offered it back then in Fort Dodge. He thought he knew what birth was. He had seen a dog give birth once behind his parents' store, and once, on a farm outside Sioux City, he saw a pig giving birth, but he had no idea what the relationship was between *oxygen* and *birth*. And what did Freund mean when he said "it seems"? Didn't he know? Wasn't he there? What was Neal paying him for? Neal looked at Rita's face. It was ashen, but her eyes were open, hooked to the blank wall opposite her. He touched her arm with one hand and with the other, caught the doctor's next sentence.

"He suffered a brain hemorrhage at birth."

Strike two. Here was the connection, but what was this fucking bastard telling them? "What do you mean?" Neal said, his voice wavering between fear and rage. These weren't numbers. Freund was in a different ballpark, a foreign league. Rita didn't move or twitch. Neal felt more alone than ever. "Do you mind if I have a smoke?" Neal said, taking a Camel out of his shirt pocket without offering one to the doctor. He put it in his mouth but didn't light it.

Freund moved to the window behind Neal. Neal turned toward him. The sky was almost cloudless. Freund suddenly turned around to face them.

"I'm afraid your son is brain damaged," he said, one hand in each of the large pockets of his white coat.

In the silence that followed, Neal imagined holding not a mitt or a bat but two pistols, one in each hand. With one he aimed at Freund, with the other at the words released into the air like scared birds.

"Brain . . . damaged." The words tasted bitter. Still, he tried to make sense of them during the lengthening silence. He knew what a brain was. Didn't know how the damn thing worked, but nobody did. His father used to tell him that Jews had strong ones, a *Yiddishe kopf*, he called it, but from Neal's experience, he wouldn't swear that was true. He knew what damage was, having been in a semitrailer in a ditch, on its side. He could estimate damage from the smell of rotten eggs, the stench of spoiled butter, damaged goods that ate away his income on a monthly basis. But what in God's name was brain damage? Was his son a retard? A mongoloid? His sixth-grade teacher used to tell him, "Neal, you have a brain, but it's damaged." Was that a genetic assessment? Stupidity—his or hers? Or plain anti-Semitism?

Neal rubbed his hands over his bare head.

"What in the name of Christ are you talking about, Dr. Freund?"

"I can't tell you a whole lot more," Freund said. "It's too early to know. We'll know more as he grows . . . if he grows."

Fucking bastard. Neal wanted to throw the bottle of ammonia under the sink in the corner of the room. He wanted to punch his fist through the innocent window, crack his own skull and then Freund's against the strangling wall. *You bastard*, he wanted to say. *You filthy stinkin' lousy smartass white-coated doctor SOB OB.*

He looked at the sky. One weak lone cloud hung immobile in the vast blue, balancing on the line of trees along East Boulevard. A baby chick with two heads. In a flash Neal understood. There had been a major foul.

* * *

Beth, with the pitying look on her face, walked into the room, nodded to Freund, and pulled back the blanket covering Rita and shoved a thermometer under her tongue. The conversation stopped while the nurse took Rita's pulse and wrote the numbers on the chart hanging at the end of the bed. Beth looked at the doctor. "Sorry to interrupt," she said.

She was an accomplice. They were the winning team; he and Reet, the losers. Neal only had two pistols, but Freund had a whole arsenal.

Rita looked comatose. Neal collapsed into his chair. This was the Mount Zion, beloved of the Lord? It felt more like Hell, with he and Rita locked and tortured in its gates.

"Talk to me simple, Doc. Gimme a for instance," Neal said, staring at the green piqué blanket again, eyes open, his voice calm but inside wanting to run away, to drive a semitrailer to Saint Paul or farther, even to Fargo.

Freund moved away from the window and back to his chair on the other side of Rita's bed. As he walked he told them that it *could* be that the baby might be blind.

Neal held on to the "could" and "might," knowing Freund could have said "would." There was hope. Neal closed his eyes. "Go on," he told Freund, settling into a state in which he could catch whatever the doctor threw. Rita was alive. That was the most important thing. Hell, he knew that some women died during childbirth. Or the baby.

"It could be that he'll be deaf."

The man was a sadist, *could* or no *could*. Neal didn't need any more proof. He put his hand on Rita's shoulder, more to balance himself than comfort her. She seemed beyond comfort, her eyes closed, her breath barely audible.

"It could be . . .," Freund began again, as if he were just warming up, "it could be his motor development will be impaired." Rita's eyes opened and she turned toward Neal, staring not at him but through him. "I know how devastating this is for you, Rita and Neal," Freund said.

Now he was talking from a different place in the field. It wasn't just could bes. He felt their pain. Or so he said. How could he possibly feel their pain?

He was explaining that loss of oxygen at birth is rare, but it happens. "What most families do after a few months," he said, "is place their babies in a home for special children." He waited a minute before he began again. "If you're lucky, they usually die within the first six months." Freund coughed. "A year at the most."

His words fell onto Rita's blanket, each one pushing her deeper into herself. Neal's hands and legs felt numb.

"The best advice anyone can give you," Freund said as he slowly stood up, "is to get pregnant again, as soon as possible."

Air attacks. Machine guns. The whole fucking armed forces aimed at their hearts. The motherfucker in command, who may have botched the birth, versus Neal, sitting defenseless like an idiot, dreaming of a first son, and Rita, the mother, devastated into immobility. The guy could have fed this to them in bits and pieces, but no, he used his entire arsenal in less than five minutes. Was this what Neal had demanded? Now he felt guilty for his behavior last night. Maybe if he hadn't been so stubborn, Freund would have stopped with "could be blind."

Neal stood up, bent over Rita, and kissed her cheeks. Then he kissed her eyes. He whispered, "We'll deal with this later." Somehow they would manage, he told her. "The important thing is that you are alright, the girls are fine, and we'll get through this, together, somehow." He didn't say "just like other couples" because he didn't know any other couples with "special children." He put his hand under her blanket and fished around for her hand, assuming there would be more bad news from Dr. Freund. "It might be okay," he said, trying to believe his own words.

Freund stood by the bed in silence. Neal caught him checking his watch. Then he went to the sink and brought Rita a paper cup of water, handing it to Neal to give to her. Neal held the rim of the cup against Rita's lower lip, told her to open her mouth, but instead she pushed his hand away. The water spilled all over the bed and the cup fell to the floor.

Neal imagined the waters receding. He wanted to go back to the kitchen table. He wanted the script to stop five minutes before the deluge. She could still be before the birth, just resting in the hospital, even for a month. He could cope. The little fella needed another month in the womb.

His eye caught the headline on the chair. "I'm not selling the Indians," said Veeck. "These people are buying them. By that I mean I am making no active effort to sell."

Nothing made sense. Everything was cockeyed. His son, a foul ball.

* * *

The whole staff knew about the Stonehill baby and kept their distance. How else could he explain the nurse down on the fourth floor in charge of preemies pushing her chair back from the desk as he leaned over the counter to ask for directions? She couldn't walk him to the room? She had to point? Did they think it was catching, whatever his son had? Maybe the father was brain damaged too? Even the lady at the newsstand this morning took three steps back when he bought the paper. He hadn't thought anything of it then. But now, as this feeling of being different, damaged, began to weigh on him, he remembered the elevator man. The guy didn't give him the time of day. And Nurse Beth, when she took Rita's vital signs, no congratulations. Not even a smile. Hell, when Judy had been born even the cleaning woman said congratulations. Now they reacted as if a sign were written across his forehead: "BEWARE, Father of Vegetable Baby."

He walked to the window and pushed the cotton curtain aside. The room of incubators for the preemies looked more like a factory than a nursery. Nine plastic boxes—or were they glass crates?—sat on metal stands, a baby inside each one. Pipes coiled under each incubator, and more pipes led from them to the babies, in and out of the room. He had seen something like this before. Where was it? Chicago. Yes. 1934. He had spent a summer afternoon at the World's Fair, watching the girlie show on the midway. On the way out a man called to him, "Don't miss the babies! Come see the amazing preemies!"

The barker succeeded in arousing his curiosity. He paid the five cents and stepped behind a heavy black curtain to see "the show": twelve babies in incubators. They were like the freaks of nature he had once seen at a state fair in Des Moines—a cow with five legs, the fifth growing out of its back, a pig with three tails. He wondered how the City of Chicago could allow such a thing: charging money to look at deformed babies, little human beings that could fit into your pocket. The people around him seemed to be fascinated. "Look at that one," they shouted to each other. One woman in the crowd said she came every week to see how the babies grew. Now his only son was in one of those contraptions. It broke his heart.

"Which is mine?" he called to the nurse.

"Number three," she said, looking up from her charts.

It didn't matter. There were no numbers, and he couldn't make out any distinguishing features. They all looked gruesome and, in that sense, alike. He remembered Judy's bald head and Elizabeth's matted brown hair. Their foreheads were his, their fingers Reet's. But this? This was a freak show. Now he understood why Freund hadn't been anxious for him to see his son. Neal closed the curtain and walked, head down, to the nurse.

"How the hell am I supposed to know which is mine? Do these babies have names?"

The nurse ran her red fingernail through charts.

"Show me my boy," Neal said.

"Impossible, Mr. Stonehill," she said. "Only doctors and specially trained nurses can go in there. It's controlled for temperature and germs." She took out a nail file from a drawer. "We have to keep it as sterile as possible," she added, looking up. And then, "Their names do not appear, but the doctors have a system."

"How long will he have to be in there?" His voice was on the verge of breaking into a cry.

"We're a new unit here at Mount Zion, Mr. Stonehill. This is only our third year. Most babies go home anywhere between six weeks and six months. No promises."

Neal wondered if the nurse understood that his son was different, not a normal preemie, if she knew everything Freund had told them upstairs—the oxygen, the hemorrhage. Now he wondered what exactly Freund had seen that made him draw those conclusions. Neal's heart was pounding out of his chest. A miracle the nurse didn't tell him to keep it quiet. Christ, this was a pistol. What the hell would he tell Rita and everyone else? Soon he'd have to go home and face Vashti and the girls. What would he say? Everyone was expecting good news. *Powder your face with sunshine* . . . baby's a freak and Rita's out to lunch . . . *smile, smile, smile.*

As he walked toward the elevator, he wondered if and when they would name him. Could he have a bris? He and Reet had agreed to George Joseph, but now he needed a winning name. Rita's father, George, had died when she was eight, and Joseph died alone in LA. The baby needed a winning name. Neal liked Early. Maybe Wynn had been a preemie. Look what a great pitcher he became. The baby could grow up to be just fine. Blind people functioned. They had dogs. Deaf people functioned. Look at Helen Keller. *Everything could be all right.* Of course they would give him a name.

* * *

Rita was sleeping when he walked back into room six. He lifted the paper from the floor, sat down, and read the front page. An article about some guy named Davis caught his attention. Davis had been sentenced to the electric chair in the Ohio Penitentiary for killing a Cleveland Heights policeman. The Reverend Mr. Wall followed Davis into the death chamber and read the twenty-third psalm while guards tightened the leather straps. Neal wondered if the psalm made the death less painful. He tried to recall the words, the same psalm he had recited at his father's funeral a year earlier. All he could remember was "shepherd" and "house of the Lord."

He turned to Rita, who had been sleeping when he walked in. Now she was staring at him and saying something.

"What did you say?"

Her words came out slowly, as if some inner hand were pulling them back inside. He stood up, leaned over, and kissed her forehead. "We'll call him George," he said, confused. During the following silence he watched her face. Small tears were forming in the corners of her eyes, tears fine and gentle, like snowflakes that disappear before they touch ground. He didn't know if he should mention the tears, so he just stood there and said the name again, adding his father's name this time.

"George Joseph. I saw the little fella, Reet. A real beauty." He didn't like to lie, especially to his wife, but he wanted to make her happy.

Rita closed her eyes and swallowed. When she opened them again, the tears had made them sparkle. "I need water," she said.

"Sure, sweetheart." There were no more paper cups in the dispenser, so he left the room, ran to the nurses' station, and told them his wife needed water.

The nurse on duty gave him a paper cup and told him to fill it up in the sink in the room. "This is a good sign," she said.

When he entered the room the pillow was covering Rita's face. He filled the cup with water and approached the bed.

"Come, sweetheart," he said, first putting the cup on the nightstand and then lifting the pillow. Her arms shot out from under the covers and pulled the pillow back. Neal sat down.

"Can you hear me, Reet?" He didn't wait for an answer. "I brought you a cup of water. The nurse said it's good to drink. We'll get through this, sweetheart."

He had no idea if and how they would get through whatever this was, but he knew that Rita needed to hear it and that she needed to drink.

A minute later she lifted the pillow. "Where's Daddy?" she said, her words mixed with tears.

Neal couldn't believe it. Her father had been dead twenty years, yet her voice was that of an eight-year-old child who still waited for him to come home.

"He's down on the fourth floor, sweetheart. The baby. In an incubator. I saw him. He's precious. They take good care of him down there." She placed the pillow back over her face. "Your daddy isn't coming home."

Under the blanket she still looked pregnant. How the hell were they going to survive this? Who could help? What kind of help would they need? Rita's mother was a good cook, especially when it came to Hungarian dishes. Hopefully, she could babysit a few days a week. His ma was still out in Fort Dodge, and his sisters were busy with their own growing families in Chicago. Rita's sisters were busy treading water with their own young kids. His brothers didn't know the first thing about kids. Maybe he didn't either. A situation like this, with a problematic preemie in an incubator, you didn't want to share that kind of information with too many people. A baby like this was an embarrassment.

"Let me see your face, honey."

She slowly moved the pillow so her mouth and nose were visible.

"I'll give you some more water." He picked up the cup and held it against her lips. She took a sip, still holding the pillow over her eyes. When she lay back down, she asked who he looked like.

"Who?" said Neal.

"The baby," she said, pillow still covering her eyes.

"Around the mouth, like you," he lied, "and the nose more like mine. He's fair, like my side. The nurse says he'll be a blondie."

Rita sighed. Neal thought he detected not a smile, exactly, but the wish for a smile.

"I feel ill," she said.

"You had a hard time, sweetheart. Each day you'll get stronger, and soon you'll come home."

"What about the baby?"

"What about him?" Neal said.

"Will he come home?"

"Of course he'll come home, sweetheart. He's our son."

Rita moved the pillow from her eyes. They were red and her cheeks damp. "It hurts when I cry," she said, putting her hands on her belly.

He looked into her moist eyes, two orbs that held their future. He tried to read them. Would everything be as good as it could be, or would everything fall apart? And if everything fell apart, would it be in stages or all at once? Would he be able to put the pieces together again, like he could with a broken-down truck?

"Joey," he whispered.

"That's a nice name," Rita said, then fell silent again, drifting back into herself, leaving Neal alone with unanswered questions circling his head, like the wires and pipes encircling his son two floors below.

* * *

On the fifth day after the birth, Rita began writhing from pain in her breasts. Even Neal could see they were big as udders. He couldn't figure out why the staff hadn't taken care of it earlier like they had done when the girls were born. Rita had no intention of breastfeeding, and this baby couldn't even suck. Neal walked over to the nurses' station and said to nobody in particular that his wife needed help. Nobody responded until Nurse Lenore walked around to his side of the station and asked what the problem was.

"Nursing," Neal said. "My wife isn't doing that and she needs help. She's as big as a cow."

Lenore smiled and walked back with him to Rita's room. Neal looked at her as they walked next to each other. She was the one who had told him he could go talk to Freund the night of the birth. He was glad she was on duty in maternity.

Standing next to the bed, Lenore put her hand on Reet's head and smoothed her hair, as if she knew Rita. "I understand your breasts hurt, Rita," she said in a calm, gentle voice, her lips near Reet's ear.

Rita tried to smile. This Lenore was the first ray of sunshine they'd found at Mount Zion. She promised she'd bring Rita some pills to take away the pain, and within ten minutes she had fulfilled that promise.

The next morning, when Neal was once again sitting in the chair by the window, reading the *Plain Dealer*, he heard a muffled sound. Rita was crying under her pillow. He put down the paper and stood next to the bed.

"What's wrong, sweetheart?" he said, feeling stupid as ever. Everything was wrong. They both knew that. He put his hand on her arm and started stroking it, the way Lenore had stroked her hair. She moved her other hand to the nightstand and fished around for a tissue. "I want to see . . .," she said.

"What, sweetheart? What can I get for you?" Neal's knees shook.

"I want to see my baby."

From the first day after the birth, Neal had settled into a routine of visiting Reet every day and then going down to the fourth floor to check on the baby. Once he figured out which incubator held his son, the whole thing broke his heart. He didn't know what was harder—seeing Rita crying and hiding under the pillow or seeing his son, connected to tubes and pipes, crying. He didn't know who was more helpless, the baby, his wife, or himself. Freund told him Rita would probably have to stay two weeks in the hospital for monitoring. He couldn't predict how long it would be until the baby could go home, if that was what they wanted.

Neal didn't want anyone else to see Rita like this, and he certainly did not want anyone to see the baby, so he put off work and came every day, leaving the house early in the morning and staying till after his little girls went to sleep. Thank God for Vashti and her fanny spoon and Rita's mom. When he spoke to the girls on the phone, he kept making excuses.

Now, five days after the birth, Rita wanted to see the baby. This was a good sign, but he wondered what it would do to her. Not that she would be able to see much. From the first visit to the preemie ward, when he couldn't even tell which baby was his, the nurses and doctors there had referred to his son as "a vegetable." It made him sick, but on his visits over the last three days, after one of the nurses let him in to see his son close up, he began to realize the description was appropriate. While Neal was looking at him, the baby's limbs turned stiff and rigid and his back arched. He looked frozen, as if he would never get out of that arch. A frozen green bean. He didn't want Rita to see this yet, not when she could barely sit up and smile.

So when, on the fifth day, Rita expressed an interest in seeing the baby, Neal explained to her that according to the rules at Mount Zion, parents could only stand behind a glass window for the first visit. If she really wanted to, he would take her down to the fourth floor, but his advice would be for her to wait a few days, until she had built up her strength by walking around the sixth floor.

By day nine she was ready. Neal held her by the elbow as they walked toward the elevator. On the ride down Rita leaned into the corner. Once on the ward, they both nodded as they walked past the nurses' station. Some of the nurses, who had watched Neal every day as he walked to and from the preemie room, gave him the familiar pitying look. Now, more than anger, he felt heartbreak.

Neal stopped in front of the cotton curtain.

"Where is he?" Rita asked.

"Are you ready?" he said, almost hoping she would change her mind. She nodded. He pushed back the curtain with his left hand, putting his right around Reet's shoulders.

Rita gasped and collapsed into his side. He held her with both arms. "It's okay, sweetheart. They're taking good care of him in there. He's nice and warm."

She turned her face into his chest and asked that he shut the curtain. "Take me back," she said. Her body sunk into his. "Now," she begged.

That afternoon, as Freund made his rounds, Neal caught him outside Rita's room and asked him for some easy medical term to apply to the baby. Was he retarded? A mongoloid? He had to tell their families something but didn't know how. Freund hit him with "intracranial hemorrhage," "hydrocephalus," "periventricular tonic convulsions," "clonic movements," and a list of other unpronounceable and incomprehensible medical terms that were anything but easy.

Neal lost his temper and challenged Freund, charging that he himself had caused the foul. "Where were you when the baby needed oxygen?"

Freund turned and headed down the hall without answering.

Neal shouted after him, "No, tell me. Where were you?"

Freund turned around and said three words: "Congenital spastic paralysis."

Lenore came walking toward Neal and ushered him into Rita's room. She moved quickly to Rita and advised Neal that arguing in the hospital wasn't good for anyone, especially not his wife. Neal took a Camel and matches from his pocket and lit up.

Lenore, one hand rubbing Rita's head, asked if they wanted to know what congenital spastic paralysis meant.

Neal was surprised when Rita nodded.

"It's a form of paralysis," she began, as if describing a faraway land. Neal couldn't imagine what it looked like. There had been a paralyzed boy in Fort Dodge, always in a wheelchair. Neal saw him every summer at the town's swimming hole. He sat in his wheelchair and watched the other kids swim. Neal remembered feeling sorry for him.

Lenore continued. "What happens is that the part of the nervous system that controls coordinated movements, movements like you and I make"—she lifted her arms above her head to demonstrate—"is disabled. So the child cannot move in a coordinated manner. You'll see a lot of spasmodic muscle contractions."

Neal and Rita looked at each other. Neither of them seemed to know how to respond. Neal wanted to know if there was a cure. Rita didn't say a word.

"Congenital spastic paralysis." Neal practiced saying the words a few times between long drags from his cigarette. The term could have been Hebrew for all he knew, but still, it sounded medical, unlike *vegetable*, and thus, maybe, curable.

* * *

On Saturday, July 2, 1949, Neal was told he could take Rita home the next day. The baby would have to stay in the incubator. Neal and Rita could visit daily between two and three fifteen.

After breakfast on Sunday, Lenore helped Reet put on her hot-pink muumuu that he had brought from home while Neal took care of all the paperwork. When he returned to room six, Lenore was sitting on the bed and Rita was in the chair by the window, beautiful in her muumuu with the Hawaiian flowers. Maybe they'd be able to go there, someday, to Hawaii. He wanted to take her far away from Mount Zion.

"You take good care of her, Mr. Stonehill," Lenore said. She stood up, put a hand on Neal's shoulder, and looked at Rita. "She's one beautiful lady."

Neal thanked her for her help and kindness.

Lenore bent down and gave Rita a hug. "Take care, now, sweetheart. We'll look after your little boy."

"Thank you, Lenore . . . for everything," Rita said. Neal was flabbergasted. He hadn't heard her speak to anyone in the hospital the whole time she was there.

Neal helped Rita stand up, and the three of them walked to the elevator, Neal's left arm around Reet's shoulders, his right carrying her overnight case. The floor was quiet, for which Neal was grateful. Lenore waved to them once they were in the elevator, and Rita blew her a kiss.

As they walked by the information desk on the entrance level, Neal looked up at the sign: "God loves the Gates of Zion." He shook his head. Had the past two weeks been an expression of God's love? Neal did not share his questions with Rita, who walked carefully next to him, holding his arm and her own world of questions tightly inside. When they reached the car, Rita leaned against the passenger door while Neal shoved the suitcase into the trunk. Once in the car, she put on her sunglasses, even though it was cloudy.

"Expecting rain," Neal said, turning on the ignition. He backed out and drove onto East 105th.

"Good," she said. Her hands sat locked in her lap. He wondered if she was praying. He imagined her collapsing onto the rubber mat under the glove compartment. Good that he had cleaned the car yesterday. It took all the willpower he could muster not to light up a Camel.

"Why do they call it Mount Zion?" she said, smoothing her muumuu over her belly as if it were a wrinkled baby blanket.

"I don't know, honey. There's some quote up there on the wall about deliverance."

The road was clear, less traffic than during the week. People were in church, probably, or preparing for their Fourth of July picnics. He passed a slow driver in front of him and scooted over to Chester. "Maybe the Jewish founders wanted to feel close to Jerusalem. Why do you ask?"

"I don't know."

He asked again how she felt.

"Tired," she said.

From the corner of his eye he saw her looking at the orange roof of Howard Johnson's. "Want a cone?" He felt his heart skip a beat and wondered if this sensation he was feeling, what he called worry, might be what Perry Como and Dinah Shore called love. He had felt it as a kid whenever he was around newborn puppies or kittens. He had felt it with Rita on their first skate, and again during their honeymoon in Sioux City. He felt it after Elizabeth was born, but he hadn't felt it in some time, what with being on the road so much and all the commotion with two little girls, a lousy pregnancy, and now this. But now, when his heart felt unbalanced, off kilter, he felt it again. Calling it love made him glow from inside. He wanted to let Rita know how much he loved her, despite the fact that their spastic baby was lying in a plastic box in Mount Zion. At least she, his wife and the mother of their little girls, was coming home.

"Want a cone?" he repeated.

"No," she said. She wanted to go home and go to sleep.

"You're my sweetheart, you know," he said, his eyes on the road as he drove up Fairhill. "You know that, don't you?"

Ten minutes later when they pulled into the garage on Ludlow, Rita let out a long sigh and rolled up her window. "Oh, that smell." Again she locked her hands together and bent her head. This time Neal was sure she was praying.

"What gives?" he said.

"That nurse, Lenore. She told me whenever I felt low or empty or scared, I should hold my hands like this, close my eyes, and pray."

Neal kept his mouth shut until he thought he'd explode. His wife was so gullible. "That's good, honey. Now I'll get your bag out of the trunk. We'll take the stairs real slow."

"Did you tell the girls?" she said.

"About what?" He was standing outside the car, waiting, and she was still sitting in the passenger seat, praying. He could smell the accumulated fumes from the car, mixed with cigarette smoke. He wanted to get out of the goddamned garage. "Come on, sweetheart, let's go."

"About the baby," she said, so slowly he barely understood.

"Of course not," he said, and then regretted his tone. "I mean, what can they understand about these things?" He spotted the lawnmower leaning against the far wall and thought he'd use it later in the day, while Rita was sleeping.

"What did you tell Mom?"

Or maybe he would go play a few holes at Highland. "I told her the little fella is in an incubator, that we don't know when he'll come home."

Now she was standing up outside the car in the garage, one hand balanced on the roof of the car. "What did she say?"

"She asked me what an incubator was," he said, "so I tried to explain it to her."

Rita's chest seemed to deflate. He felt bad for telling her the truth right before they went inside. Christ, she hadn't seen the girls in two weeks and her own mom in more than three. He would have to think more before he opened his mouth, which was exactly what his sixth-grade teacher had told him. The last thing Neal wanted to do now was to make Rita feel worse than she already did.

She walked out of the garage. He took out the suitcase and stood it next to her. With a tug, he pulled down the garage door, and then he lifted her suitcase. The moment was now in front of him, like an elephant, but he still tried to avoid it. "You sure you don't want to go for ice cream first?" he said, hoping she would understand his dread of going home without a baby—no wicker basket, no blue blanket, no pacifier, no thrill, no heart stretched to bursting, no taking in the fleshy reality of being the father of three. He felt a knotted void inside and wondered if it was the kind of emptiness Lenore had described, a void that could be filled by folded hands and prayer. He never prayed. What would he say, and to whom? Dear God, save my son? Was that what he wanted? The truth wasn't so clear.

He wanted to stop the clock on June 17. He wanted to erase the past two weeks. He doubted any god could work that kind of magic. Only a miracle could save them now, and that miracle would be Lenore calling tonight and saying there had been a dreadful mistake at Mount Zion.

The baby we thought was yours actually belongs to the woman who gave birth next to Rita. Your baby is one hundred percent healthy!

He opened the back door and, turning to Rita, both of them standing in the July afternoon heat, said, "Welcome home."

She attempted a smile. He lifted the suitcase with one hand and placed the other on Rita's back as she climbed the stairs, resting after every two or three, leaning against the wall, breathing deeply. When they reached the landing opposite the closed kitchen door, he put down the suitcase and gave her a hug. She moaned and pushed him away.

* * *

The kitchen was empty, but within ten seconds the little one ran in and jumped on Rita, screaming, "Mommy, Mommy, you're home!" Her shouts brought Elizabeth running into the kitchen, followed by Rita's mom, her sewing things dangling from her apron pockets.

Neal swatted Judy's head with the back of his hand and told her to stop the commotion. "Don't you see your mother's tired? She just got home from Mount Zion. Leave her alone."

Judy froze, staring at her mother's belly. "Where's Melon?" she murmured, turning her head to her grandma.

"Who's Melon, sweetie?" Rita asked.

"She means Lemon," Neal said. "Once I told her about Bob Lemon. Thought we'd call the little fella Bob."

Rita ruffled Judy's blond hair, an attempt, Neal thought, to lessen the damage he had caused by swatting her. Elizabeth moved closer to her mother and leaned her head against Rita's arm.

"The baby," Rita said, "your new brother . . . we left the sweet little thing at Mount Zion . . ." She paused and looked at Neal for help. "So he can grow big and strong."

Neal was glad she seemed normal. Maybe she would be all right and they *would* get through this.

"Welcome home, Mommy," Elizabeth said, placing the fingers of her right hand between her mother's fingers.

"How's my big girl?" Rita said, kissing her head. "Did you help Vashti and Grandma and Daddy while I was away?"

"Yes, Mommy," Elizabeth said, patting her mother's sleeve.

"I folded laundry, but"—she pointed at Judy—"she won't stop sucking her thumb. And she cries when she has to go to sleep. Do I *have* to share a room with her?"

Neal winced. He didn't want to discuss this stuff now. He wanted to play golf or at least mow the lawn, but first he had to get Reet settled in their bed. "Okay, now that's enough, girls," he said. "Your mom is tired."

Rita's mother, Ella, who had been leaning against the kitchen sink and watching the homecoming in silence, now came over to Rita and gave her a kiss on her cheek. They stood there, mother and daughter, near the kitchen door, Rita a head taller than her mom. Neither of them spoke. They just stood looking at Elizabeth and Judy. Neal felt tense. He didn't want his Hungarian mother-in-law to start making a scene, crying, wiping her nose on her apron strings, or telling some cockamamie story about how Franz Joseph had been good to the Jews, and therefore he and Reet should name the baby Franz Joseph. Ella was one unpredictable Hungarian. Usually she was cold and distant, and she kept her mouth shut. Sometimes when she'd say something from out in left field, all hell broke loose, with the girls giggling their heads off. He hated giggling. Best to stop the homecoming now before things got out of hand. "Okay, that's enough," he said.

"Glad you're home, Rita," Ella said as she stood back and let Neal take over.

"What are you working on, Mom?" Rita said, pointing to the pieces of cotton in her mother's apron pocket and the thimble on her finger.

"Another apron. This one for you, with the forsythias you like and the deep pockets."

Rita smiled, but Neal sensed the smile might end in a sob. He put his right hand on her back and directed her out of the kitchen. They walked down the dark-green hallway to their bedroom, her suitcase in his hand, Ella and the girls following them. In the room Rita plopped onto her side of the bed. Neal bent down and took off her shoes. "I'll bring you a cold root beer."

"I want some too," Judy piped up. "Let's have a party. Mommy's home!"

Elizabeth pushed her elbow into Judy's side and told her to be quiet. "Mommy's sick," she whispered.

"No," Rita stammered.

"She's not sick," Neal said, as if handing down the law. "Mommy's tired."

Ella put a hand on each of the little girls' shoulders and pressed, holding them in place.

"Mommy, can I climb into bed with you?" Judy wiggled out of her grandmother's hold, sat on the floor, and untied her shoes. "Can we have a picnic for July Fourth? Vashti says it's important."

Neal pulled up the little one from under her arms, placed her in a standing position, turned her around to face him, and told her to leave her mother alone. "She needs rest. Can't you understand that?"

Neal went to the kitchen and brought back a glass of cold root beer with a straw. He put it on Rita's nightstand. All four of them—his daughters, mother-in-law, and himself—stood next to the bed staring at Rita in her

Hawaiian muumuu. Her soft brown curls spread over her pillow like the wicker of their laundry basket, like the weave of coils and pipes among the incubators at Mount Zion, a place that now felt like a continent, no, a planet away.

"I want a straw too," the little one whined.

Neal asked Ella to take the girls to the playroom upstairs. "All out," he said, and Ella grabbed the little girls' hands and pulled them out of their parents' bedroom without anyone saying goodbye.

* * *

Over the next two months, with the help of Ella and Vashti, Rita inched back to herself. One Saturday she baked chocolate chip cookies with Elizabeth and Judy. That was the first time Neal went to hit a few golf balls over at Highland. She started doing a little shopping at the A&P on Larchmere and even went with Ella to get her hair done at Tony's on Shaker Square. Almost every night the family sat together at the kitchen table for meat, mashed potatoes, and green beans, followed by red Jell-O or vanilla junket.

On Monday and Thursday afternoons, Neal and Reet drove down to Mount Zion to see their son. He was gaining—a hopeful sign the nurses said—but still needed to remain in the incubator. The hospital allowed them to stand next to Joey's incubator. Dressed in the hospital's white sterile robes and masks, they watched the convulsions when his limbs went rigid and his back arched, the jerky movements of his arms and legs, and strangest of all, heard his eerie, high-pitched cry.

Every two hours nurses gave Joey a bottle. Sometimes the feeding took thirty minutes because his sucking reflex was still poor. On one visit Rita expressed the desire to hold him, but the nurse refused. It was enough they let the parents stand next to the incubator. Neal hated the regulations but didn't say anything. He was grateful they could at least see him up close. What a beautiful baby he was. The pale fuzz on his head would certainly develop into blond hair like the little one's. His pale complexion reminded them of Neal's side of the family, from the Pale of Settlement, and the broad forehead that of Reet's father as a young man. The baby's eyes were a gorgeous sea blue. It broke Neal's heart to see his helpless little boy.

On the way home from these visits, Rita sat close to the passenger door, her hands covering her face. She never cried out loud. When they got home, Rita went straight to their room and closed the door. Watching the nurses feed and handle Joey through all the tubes and wires of the incubator and listening to the occasional words of Dr. Kyman, Joey's pediatrician, and Dr. Baumoel, the baby's neurologist, had an ill effect on Rita.

Instead of "vegetable," and "congenital spastic paralysis," the medical staff now referred to the baby's condition as a severe case of cerebral palsy—CP. The letters reminded Neal of DP. Displaced person suited Joey, his only home an incubator.

In September 1949, when Joey was two and a half months old, Elizabeth started kindergarten at Ludlow School and the little one started nursery school at Miss Brunner's three mornings a week. With Vashti working for them four full days a week and Ella accepting Neal's invitation to move in with them permanently—"You can have the upstairs playroom," he had told her—the family had made it through the summer.

At the beginning of October, during one of their visits at Mount Zion, Dr. Kyman took Neal aside and told him that by the end of the month, if Joey kept gaining, he could leave the hospital. Joey would probably remain blind and deaf, but he wouldn't sign on that yet. The baby's sucking reflex was continually improving. Medications were available for controlling the spasms. They would have to play around with them to see which ones worked. "Call the CP folks, too," Kyman said. "Unfortunately, they have a lot of experience." Before leaving the ward, the doctor put his hand on Neal's shoulder and said, as if an afterthought, "Your son might be better off in an institution."

Neal couldn't believe it. They had gone through all this—a lousy pregnancy, a botched birth, a brain hemorrhage, and three and a half months in an incubator—to give up their baby, their beautiful Joey?

"What do you mean?" Neal said. Kyman ignited his anger like Freund. "He's our only son, Dr. Kyman. How can we send him to an institution?"

"It's hard, Neal. You know how hard it is with healthy babies, like Elizabeth and Judy. This will be a thousand times harder. It will sap all your energy. Babies like this demand attention all day and night. Can you handle that? Can Rita? You'll need at least one nurse to help out during the nights so you two can get some rest. I've seen this before, Neal. That's why these places exist, to save families like yours."

"Families like yours?" Was there something wrong with his family? That a forty-seven-year-old man had a twenty-eight-year-old wife? Who needed saving? Elizabeth was happy in her first month at kindergarten, and the little one went to nursery school a few times a week with no problems. So what the hell was he talking about?

Rita walked over and took hold of Neal's arm. Kyman looked at her and continued. "I was just telling Neal, Rita, that by the end of October, if the baby keeps gaining, you can take him home. It will be a grind. Trust me on this one. You'll need at least one nurse."

"We want to take him home," Neal said to Kyman. Rita squeezed his arm. Neal's only concern, though he didn't mention it in front of Reet, was whether she would be able to handle Joey's lack of response. Wasn't the greatest joy of parenting having your baby smile at your voice and your touch? Joey didn't even smile, not yet. If he continued to be blind, if his cry stayed high pitched, if he couldn't hug, how would she feel? How long could she endure that?

It was too early to tell. He would help out as much as he could. Of course they would get a nurse for the nights. Thank God Ella was in place up in the playroom and handled the stairs with no problem. The little one would double up with Elizabeth in the far bedroom next to the kitchen, and Joey would get Judy's room opposite their bedroom. No doubleheaders at the stadium, not yet, but they would manage, somehow.

It wasn't only Joey who was "special," a word the medical staff used to describe their baby. Shaking Kyman's hand and thanking him for his concern, Neal realized his whole family now carried this description as well.

* * *

On Friday, October 28, 1949, at exactly two in the afternoon, one hundred and thirty-two days after his birth, George Joseph "Joey" Stonehill, weighing in at eleven and a half pounds, came home from Mount Zion Hospital. He was dressed in a blue-and-white woolen baby suit that covered his hands, and a matching white hat with blue embroidery. His little body was wrapped in a blue woolen blanket and then covered with a blue, yellow, and white quilt boasting seven ducks, which had been sewn by Ella Grossman, his maternal grandmother. His wrappings took up more room in the family's wicker laundry basket than the little thing himself. The basket sat on the back seat of the Chrysler, while the parents, Rita and Neal, sat in the front.

Neal carried the basket aloft in his arms up the back stairs, slowly and carefully. Joey didn't make a peep. Father and son were followed by the beautiful young mother and wife, Rita Fay Grossman Stonehill, who, Neal was calculating, would celebrate her twenty-ninth birthday in five weeks. At the top of the stairs, Neal stopped and took a deep breath. He wanted to tell her how overcome with emotion he was, how glad he felt that now, no matter what, their son was a living part of their family, how grateful he was for their own good health, and how much he wanted to pray, or plead, for someone to make sure they would survive the coming months and years. He wanted to say all this and more, but he knew he was not a man of words, he did not know how to say these things that seemed so strong and deep, confusing and frightening, and so, holding his one and only son in the wicker basket in front of him, he gave Rita a sheepish smile, stepped to one side of the door, and motioned to her with his balding gray head to open it.

* * *

The smell of warm pumpkin pie captured Neal as soon as the door opened. Two large pies with woven crusts sat on a rack on top of the stove. Vashti must have remembered it was his favorite. Neal hoped they were both for the family. Sometimes Vashti baked double and took half home. He walked to the kitchen table and placed the wicker basket at his end. Carrying Joey up two flights of stairs had been a strain. Neal pulled out his chair and plopped down. The TV blared from the living room. He figured the girls were lying on the floor in front of it, like usual. He turned toward them.

"Come meet your brother," he called to them in a gruff whisper.

Rita entered the kitchen behind Neal and sat in her chair at her end of the table.

Elizabeth and the little one ran into the kitchen like the wild horses they were watching on Roy Rogers.

"Where is he? Where is he?" the little one yelled, climbing onto her chair and taking a handful of the Halloween candy corn from the bowl in the middle of the table. Neal told her to calm down. "Your brother is sleeping, sweetie." Some of her candy corn dropped onto the table. Elizabeth, standing next to her mother, picked up the renegade pieces and put them in her mouth.

"He's under those blankets, right, Daddy?" Elizabeth said.

"Can we make a jack-o'-lantern for the baby?" the little one asked. "At Miss Brunner's we have a jack-o'-lantern with a light bulb inside."

"Let's talk quietly now," Neal warned, but it was too late. Joey began to whimper, and soon he was crying his terrible high-pitched cry. The girls covered their ears with their hands. Rita and Neal looked at each other, while Elizabeth and Judy looked from one parent to the other. Finally, Rita stood up, took the blankets off Joey, and lifted him ever so gently from the wicker basket. She looked as if she were holding someone else's baby, or a wounded puppy that didn't belong to her.

First she cradled Joey in her arms and looked at his face. His blue eyes were closed. Then she tickled his chin with her right index finger. "Kootchy-koo," she said, with more hope than love. Joey opened his sea-blue eyes. Tears nestled in their corners. Neal didn't think the baby was focusing on Reet as she moved her face closer to his and said, "Hi there, Joey . . . sweet Joey . . . my little Joey. Meet your sisters . . . Welcome home."

Elizabeth and Judy stood in silence, watching their mother mother their new brother. Joey cried. The sounds seemed to come from Mars, not from his tiny mouth. The little one crawled under the table to stand next to her mother. "He looks like a bird," she said, and started to giggle. "He sounds like a bird too, a mockingbird. Miss Brunner said—"

Neal told her to be quiet. She climbed onto another chair and stood up to get a better view.

"Sit down right now," Neal snapped. "Whoever told you you could stand on a chair?"

She sat down. Elizabeth moved closer to her mother to look at the baby. "He looks like spaghetti," she said.

"Where did you learn that kind of talk, Elizabeth?" He itched his head with his fist. "Is that what they teach you in kindergarten?"

"Look at his arms, Daddy. They're floppy like spaghetti," Elizabeth said.

The little one started to sing. "Found a meatball, found a meatball, found a meatball one day, one day—"

"Be quiet," Neal shouted. "Just look at your new brother and keep your mouths shut."

He helped himself to a few pieces of candy corn and moved to stand behind Rita. He played peekaboo with Joey over her right shoulder. "Peekaboo, peekaboo," he said again and again, until the girls left the kitchen table and ran back to the television set, their hands filled with candy.

Rita suggested taking Joey to his room. Neal walked behind her through the kitchen, down the dark-green hallway, and into the baby's room. It looked like a funhouse at an amusement park. Playful red animals scampered helter-skelter on the wallpaper, blocked only by a crib, changing table, window, door, and large wooden rocking chair. Rita laid Joey on the changing table and began to undress him. His crying got louder. Neal tried to give him a pacifier, but he refused with fierce movements of his head from left to right.

"There, there," said Rita, trying to calm her son with her soft voice. "That's a good little baby."

Joey kept crying. Rita removed his hat. The gentleness of her hands on the baby's head made Neal choke up. He thought of the Christmas cookies she made every year for his truckers, how she arranged them with delicacy on white doilies in little straw baskets filled with red and green cellophane. He was so grateful and proud of her. Would she be able to do that again this year, he wondered, watching her handle Joey for the first time.

The front doorbell rang. Neal went to the living room and pressed the buzzer. The chilly October air rushed up the stairs, along with a tub of a woman dressed in a long fur coat.

"My name's Pam," she said, her eyes focused on the carpeted stairs. When she reached the top, she took off her leather gloves, blew on her hands, and extended her right toward Neal, which he shook as she said, "I'm your nurse."

With his free hand Neal closed the front door behind him so the girls in the living room wouldn't hear.

"I thought you were coming *after* Halloween," Neal said, unsure if it was his mistake or hers.

"No. This is what the agency told me. Today's the twenty-eighth, right?" She took out a handkerchief from the big white canvas bag strapped over her shoulder and blew her nose.

Neal stepped back and stood against the door. "Yes," he said. It was one thing to talk theoretically about bringing in a night nurse, but here was a real one, almost the size of the landing, in the middle of the afternoon.

"Congenital spastic paralysis, right?" she said, looking at some letter in her purse. "I have eight, almost nine years' experience working with CSP, Mr. Stonehill. Your son will be in good hands."

"Pat?" he said.

"Pam," she corrected, loosening the string under her chin from her fur hat and shaking her graying mane free. "Where can I hang my coat?"

The husband side of him wanted to push this battle-axe down the stairs and roll her down the street like a snowball. The father side wanted her to do just what she was doing—take charge, show competence and confidence. She was not scared or cowed by their special baby. Neal opened the cedar closet in the hall, hung up her coat and hat, and then opened the door to the living room.

"Elizabeth, Judy, turn that thing down," he said. "I want you to meet someone."

Elizabeth stood up first and turned down the sound. They both faced their father.

"This here is Pam, and she'll be helping us with Joey," he said.

"Hi. I'm Elizabeth," said the eldest, "and this is Judy. She sucks her thumb."

The little one put her thumb in her mouth and sucked hard.

"Take that damn thing out of your mouth," Neal said.

She took it out to ask if she could watch Molly Goldberg tonight, but Neal was already leading Pam to Joey's room.

When they walked in, Rita was trying to arrange a diaper on Joey. The baby's arms and legs were flapping all over the place, as if he were doing the back crawl in a pool and was about to drown.

"Here, let me do that for you," Pam said, and without waiting for a response from Rita, pulled the diaper this way and that, stuck both ends underneath the folds without using one safety pin, slipped on some outfit over his head, snapped the buttons one two three, and lifted the little package onto her pillow of a chest.

"Who is this, Neal?" Rita asked, stepping back from the changing table with an energy Neal hadn't seen in months.

Neal introduced them, said there had been a mix-up or a misunderstanding. Apparently, Pam would be helping them five days a week, from four in the afternoon till midnight, when another nurse from the agency would come until eight in the morning. This was what the folks at Mount Zion had recommended, Neal explained, based on their experience of caring for Joey during his first four and a half months.

Rita pursed her lips and gave Neal a dazed, angry look.

"We all have lots of experience with congenital SP," Pam said, looking through Joey's drawers for a sweater. "It's pretty much like CP when you come right down to it."

"Well, Miss Pam," Rita said, raising her voice, "we don't call him SP and we don't call him CP. He has a name, our son, and his name is Joey."

Neal was stunned. He looked at Reet. This was his wife?

"Sure, Mrs. Stonehill," Pam said, rubbing Joey's back in steady circular motions as she surveyed the room. "Where's the bassinette?"

Neal and Rita looked at each other, each asking the other whether this Pam was a curse or a blessing, a dark hole or the road to salvation. Once Pam put the baby in the crib, Neal suggested they all go to the kitchen for some coffee and fresh pumpkin pie. Rita said she wanted to stay with Joey, but then walked into her room alone. Neal led Pam to the kitchen table, where they sat and went over the details of Pam's employment. He liked this Pam. They both liked Vashti's luscious pumpkin pie.

* * *

Pam bathed and fed Joey five evenings a week and put him to sleep at eight sharp. When he fussed and cried, which was always, she was right there, rubbing his back and holding him tightly against her big chest. The other nurse, who arrived at midnight and stayed till eight, was Sashay, "Like in square dancing," she had said the first time she came. Neal didn't know if she was French, Spanish, or American Indian. She slept on the rocking chair when Joey managed to sleep, and when he cried, which was often, she went through the same routine as Pam, though her chest was bonier. Pam and Sashay enabled Neal and Rita to sleep through the nights.

Ella got Elizabeth ready for kindergarten every morning, sent her off at eight thirty, and greeted her at twelve fifteen when she returned for lunch. She prepared and fed her lunch and sent her back at twelve forty-five. Ella was in the kitchen to greet her when Elizabeth returned at three fifteen. Rita helped the little one get dressed for Miss Brunner's. Fortunately, Miss Brunner's assistant, Miss Leverne, drove a big station wagon and picked up all the nursery school children on Ludlow Road at eight thirty on Mondays, Wednesdays, and Fridays, and delivered them home by twelve fifteen. Ella took care of lunch for Judy, too. Vashti came four times a week to clean the house and do the laundry, ironing, and mangling, so Rita was free for the day.

Neal drove downtown to the creamery on Gould Court every morning at eight sharp and came home by six, in time for the family dinner. No more trucking to Tracy, Minnesota, or Des Moines. No more driving through his beloved country and stopping at godforsaken motels outside Terre Haute. Rita had laid down the law. She didn't want to be in the house without him. He had to find truckers for *all* his routes. Little girls need their fathers, she had said. She knew only too well.

On the weekends, when neither Pam nor Sashay was around, Neal took over the afternoon and night shifts, often sleeping on the rocking chair with Joey in his arms. The nurses had told Neal and Rita that the big sisters shouldn't get too close to the baby because he was highly susceptible to infections. For this reason, the door to Joey's room was often closed.

All this help in the house enabled Rita to deal with Joey from eight in the morning till four in the afternoon without feeling overwhelmed.

During November, Joey thrived—less crying, more weight—but the more he thrived, the less enthusiastic Rita became. She shared her frustration with Neal every night: how sad it was that their baby never smiled or laughed and couldn't even grasp her finger when she placed it in his hand. "He never looks at me," she said. She used "spaghetti" to describe him. Despite Neal's attempts to accentuate the positive—a turn of the baby's head when he entered his room—she could not be convinced.

On days when it didn't rain or snow, Rita bundled up Joey in four layers of warm clothes and gave him to Vashti to carry him downstairs. She didn't trust herself. Vashti locked him into the carriage. Rita walked him to Shaker Square, doing each quadrant more than once. Joey was quiet in the cold, so sometimes she'd walk up Shaker Boulevard all the way to Lee and back.

When Neal heard this, it worried him. But that was nothing compared to the worry he felt one day when Rita told him something else. "We were near Coventry, and he started to whimper and whine," she said, "you know, like he does. I turned him onto his stomach and rubbed his back, but that didn't help." She covered her face with her hands and spoke through her hands. "Then I had this idea, Neal. I could put his blanket on his head and press, even a little. It would be so easy . . . to make him stay quiet . . ."

After that, Rita had Vashti or Ella take Joey for long walks while she stayed in bed, reading *House Beautiful* and *Family Circle*.

Neal didn't want Reet to vegetate at home, so he told Ella to take Reet with her on the outings to the square. After one such outing in December, Ella came to him with a story that made him realize Joey wasn't the main problem anymore.

"We were over by Woolworth's," Ella told him while he was reading the evening paper. "We ran into Sylvia, you know, the nice woman who lives down the street. Sylvia says hello to Reet, says she's rushing into Franklin Simon's for some last-minute gifts and as soon as she disappears, Rita says to me, 'Who was that?' Can you imagine? She didn't recognize her friend and neighbor from down the street."

Neal didn't like the sound of it. Rita had also become more withdrawn with him, wouldn't let him kiss her good night, let alone get close to her body. She only wanted to read those magazines and cut out recipes she never used. According to Ella, she didn't even spend time with the girls. She yelled at them once not to open her door when it was closed. It was Ella who was doing all the work— playing Fish with Elizabeth at four and watching TV with the little one at five.

When Neal brought up the subject of Christmas cookies for his truckers and the workers down at the creamery, Rita said, "What for?" Her refusal to shop for the holidays, or to decorate the fireplace as they had done in past years with a home-made sign that read "Happy New Year," and her general retreating into herself worried him, so a week before Christmas, Neal called Freund.

"Contact Zikron," Freund said. "Best man in Northeast Ohio for this sort of thing."

Neal wanted to kick himself after the call. Hadn't Freund been the one who got them into this mess? There was a limit to how many people Neal wanted to know about Joey and the family, certainly until there was some sign from the little fella that he could lift his head, smile, or see. Neal didn't know what was worse—the embarrassment of having such a baby or that his wife was going cuckoo.

Pam, Sashay, and Vashti took four days off for Christmas. That meant Neal and Ella worked round the clock while Rita stayed in bed, coming out occasionally for dinner.

Cleveland was snowed in for five days. Fortunately, the house was well stocked. Ella cooked; the television blared in competition with Joey's cries. If the girls asked for their mom, Neal made excuses for her and forbade them, under any circumstances, to bother her. He figured Reet would eventually get bored of lying in bed and one day would appear in the living room, looking radiant, ready to continue their family life.

When Neal brought Joey to their bed, Rita held him for five minutes and then told Neal to take him back. She had decided she could not mother this baby. Neal was beside himself, as well as exhausted from caregiving all day and waking up every two hours each night.

When Pam, Sashay and Vashti returned in 1950, Neal called Zikron. "We got a tough situation here," Neal said, pleading with Zikron's secretary. Freund had used the word "depression," but Ma and his sisters had never been depressed after their births. Maybe it was a sign of the times, with all these magazines advertising these newfangled machines like mangles and dish washer-dryers and stand-alone freezers and a slew of new plastic kitchenware that promised to make life easier. Who knew what invention would be next and where it would lead? All these modern conveniences let women lie around more and get depressed.

"I'm sorry, Mr. . . ."

"Stonehill," said Neal.

"The soonest Dr. Zikron will be able to see your wife is January 18, 1950. Tuesday, at five. Do you want that appointment? It's the last one of the day."

He hated doctors and their secretaries. "We'll be there," he said. "Thanks."

More snow fell in Cleveland during the first twenty days of 1950 than in November and December of '49 put together. There was no way Neal was going to drag Rita down to Carnegie to see this crook in that weather. What if they got stuck? Neal was a good driver, the best, but the Best Location in the Nation couldn't clear the streets fast enough in blizzard conditions. At noon on the eighteenth, Neal called Zikron's office to reschedule for the following week.

"I'm so sorry, Mr. Stone, but Dr. Zikron is going to Mexico on the nineteenth, and then he's teaching out of the city from February until April twelfth. He'll be treating Cleveland patients again from the fifteenth of April."

Neal rubbed his head. Wasn't this the damnedest thing!

"Excuse me, sir. What did you say?"

"Talking to myself, miss. So give me an appointment on April sixteenth."

"I'm afraid that's impossible, Mr. Stone—"

"Stonehill," Neal shouted.

"Yes, of course. Mr. Stonehill. I'm sorry. The earliest appointment is for July fifth."

"What the hell is the matter with you people? I have a situation here." Now he didn't care who heard him. "My wife lies around all day reading magazines. Do you understand what I'm saying, miss? My two little girls think their mom's on vacation in her bedroom. She's out to lunch. Do you understand? This is no vacation. We have a baby here with CSP. Do you know what that is? Freund told me to call you folks. You have to get me an earlier appointment or we'll all go crazy."

The secretary said she understood, but it was obvious to Neal she understood nothing. "Some of our patients did get here this morning, Mr. Stonehill, despite the blizzard," she said. "Do you want to take the appointment on July fifth?"

"Yes . . . No . . . Yes," Neal said, banging his fist on the kitchen counter. "Give me the goddamned appointment on the fifth and hopefully there will be no snow and Herr Doktor will be in the city." He slammed the receiver into the cradle. The phone fell off the counter, cradle and all.

Valentine's Day came and went with no cookies. Passover came and went, with Rita sleeping through the seder at her sister's house. Even the golf tournament at Lake Forest in June did not bring her out of her slumber or depression or whatever she had that was keeping her prone. By July she wasn't even bothering to stand up and get dressed. She stayed in her nightgown all day while Vashti, Ella, Pam, Sashay, and Neal took care of Joey, who still couldn't lift his head when lying on his tummy. Kyman, the pediatrician, had determined that if he couldn't see now, after a year, then he would never see, and the same went for his hearing. All their sweet talk and gentle voices had been in vain. Even on his birthday when the girls went into Joey's room and sang the monkey song and the meatball song, it drew no response. July Fourth came, the second one in a row that the family had stayed home—no picnic, no parades, no fireworks.

Rita had agreed to go to Zikron with Neal, but he wasn't sure she would follow through. On July 5, Neal told Ella to help Rita get dressed.

Neal walked into Joey's room and knelt next to the bed so his face would be even with his son's. When Joey's eyes were closed and his body wasn't flapping, Neal liked to imagine that he could be normal, breathing just like the girls did when they were babies. Neal wanted to believe that everything might be all right, one day, maybe, that Joey would focus on the red animals scampering on the white wallpaper, would hear his family's voices, despite Dr. Kyman's prognosis. It could still happen, some miracle. It was a matter of patience and constant care. Thank God for Pam. She may be fat as a hippo, but she was full of love for their little Joey. And thank God for Sashay. This was their expertise, caring for what they called special babies, God's gifts to mankind, they called them, more often than Neal cared to hear.

Rita walked into the baby's room wearing a powder-blue sundress. Her voice sounded like she was accusing him when she asked, "What are you doing down there?" Neal stood up.

"I wanted to look at him," he said, his throat feeling suddenly tight.

"Where are you taking me?"

"Dr. Zikron. I told you."

"I don't need a doctor," his wife shot back, and she turned and left the room.

He followed her into the kitchen. She was standing in front of the fridge with the door open.

"What do you want, Reet?" Neal said.

She moved her stare from the fridge to his face. Her eyes, though cloudy, pierced him.

"I don't know," she said. Her tone made him feel guilty. "What do *you* want?"

* * *

As the elevator ascended to the seventh floor, Neal reached for Rita's hand. It felt sweaty and limp. He wondered if this Zikron doctor who traveled to Mexico and taught all over the USA was the right address for Reet. An industrial leather smell pervaded the elevator, making his nose itch. Maybe they needed a vacation in Mexico. He hated doctors. Maybe she needed a Broadway show, something colorful and light that would make her snap out of it, a musical perhaps.

When the elevator door opened, the sign hit him: "Dr. Bernard Zikron, Specialist in Psychiatry and Neurological

Disorders, PhD, MD." Letters after a name always annoyed him. Why did the guy need the fancy abbreviations? Was he so different from the other 1.7 million Americans in greater Cleveland? Neal shook his head in disgust and put his hand on Rita's back to direct her down the hall.

"Where are we?" she asked, running her hand along the rough plastered wall.

He explained again, for the umpteenth time, that Freund had suggested Reet see this Dr. Zikron about her lack of interest in anything other than *Good Housekeeping* and *Family Circle*, and her sometimes forgetting the names of friends. He opened the door and assessed the waiting room. Four people were sitting around a central coffee table, looking at their knees. There was an empty orange velvet chair in one corner, an empty folding chair and a cuckoo clock in the other. Neal led Rita to the velvet chair. She dropped into it and began to rub the armrests with gusto. A little wooden bird sprang from the stick house on the clock and chimed four times. Rita pushed herself against the back of the chair and reached for Neal's hand.

"What's that?" she asked, her eyes darting around the room.

"A cuckoo clock, sweetheart," Neal whispered, and sat down on the folding chair next to her. He watched her take the morning paper from the table and stare at the headline.

"What does it say?" she asked softly.

One man lifted his face and Neal saw a huge scar on his forehead over his left eyebrow. Was he a patient or the "accompanying adult"? That's how the secretary had defined his role for this meeting. She'd told him to read the papers she would send him before their arrival, which would explain all about the treatment. The papers sat, unread, in the inside pocket of his jacket. He had been afraid to read them. As it was, he wasn't sure he was doing the right thing bringing her to a psychiatrist-neurologist. Hell, it was their son who needed a neurologist, not his beautiful young wife. But he kept the papers and figured he'd read them during Reet's treatment.

"What does this say?" Rita asked again, pointing to the headline.

The question surprised him. Didn't she read magazines? And if not, what was she doing in bed all day?

"US cruiser sinks six Red ships, total brought to eleven in two days. Invaders of South Korea dig in." The war interested him, but he knew he wouldn't be able to concentrate on the article until Rita was inside with Zikron.

When the receptionist's window slipped open, Neal stood up and went to register.

"Miss?" he said. She smelled of Chanel No. 5. How long had it been since he had smelled Reet's favorite perfume? "I'm Mr. Stonehill. The missus is over there in the corner."

"Nice to meet you finally, Mr. Stonehill. I'm sorry it has taken so long for you and your wife to get here."

She sounded like a recording. "It's just my wife," he said.

"Dr. Zikron will be right with you."

Neal returned to his seat. "What are vaders?" Rita asked. Neal looked at the paper again.

"Invaders," he said.

Neal asked her to read to herself. Ten minutes later a nurse in a white uniform with a name badge that said "Irene Blackwell" was standing in front of Rita, introducing herself and explaining that she was going to accompany them to see Dr. Zikron now. Neal explained that Rita was the patient, he the accompanying adult, but Irene was not deterred. "Dr. Zikron wants to see both of you first," she said, as if she had said this sentence a thousand times. Rita put her hands on the armrests, digging in. The paper slipped from her lap. Neal stood up. Irene placed her arms under Rita's upper arms and lifted her off the chair.

"Take your hands off me," Rita shouted. "Who do you think you are?"

Neal started to put his hand on her arm, but Irene told him it was unnecessary. "I can handle this," she said.

"They're here to help you," Neal said, and told her to relax.

Rita flailed her arms as Irene steered her to the door leading to the inner hallway, Neal following. It still wasn't too late to take her home.

"We can come another day," he said to Irene. "It's been a tough month." Neal moved closer to Irene. "The little one gets terrible eczema on her legs and arms every summer. The baby is blind and deaf, and well, my mother in Iowa developed diabetes. Maybe—"

"Please keep your voice down, Mr. Stonehill, so we can get your wife to the doctor's office." The receptionist stood in the hallway, glaring at him. "The doctor is waiting."

Within seconds Neal and Rita were sitting in Dr. Zikron's office. It reminded Neal of Freund's office, with degrees, certificates, and awards plastered in rows all over the walls. Zikron was in his sixties, with a full head of white hair and black-rimmed glasses. He spoke with a European accent but looked like an American movie star. He wanted some information from Neal and then Neal could return to the waiting room while he treated Rita.

Zikron asked about Rita's sleep, diet, periods, social relations, mothering, previous illnesses, previous deaths in the family, inherited illnesses, and a few other things that made Neal think the guy had been through a lot. Maybe he was a survivor of the camps. Neal felt humbled and answered the questions as best he could. Rita also piped up occasionally but mainly sat with her hands held together in her lap, maybe praying, though Neal hadn't seen that for months.

When Zikron started asking about the birth and the baby, Rita slid down lower in her chair. Neal answered most of the questions the best he could. After ten minutes of this, Zikron began to explain. "ECT, electroconvulsive therapy, electroshock therapy, or simply shock treatments, as we call them now in America, could help Rita get back to mothering and functioning." Turning directly to Rita, he said, "You are an excellent candidate for this treatment, Mrs. Stonehill, and I am confident the treatments will help you feel better."

Neal reached out to hold Reet's hand. Shock therapy? Convulsive? Neal had figured Rita would get pills, maybe a shot. Hell, he thought a Broadway musical might help. Electric shocks for his wife? This was madness. How could this doctor, who seemed so civilized and educated, do such a thing? Was he a Nazi?

Fear and uncertainty caused him a moment of paralysis. Part of him wanted to stay with Rita and hold her hand, but another part wanted to go back to the chair in the waiting room and read the paper, grateful that someone else, someone with experience and knowledge, would deal with his wife.

Everything that had happened since June 18, 1949—the premature birth, the brain hemorrhage, the CSP Joey—all this was out of the ballpark of his understanding. In his wildest dreams he never could have imagined that his beautiful, vivacious young wife would become chronically sad and withdrawn. Like it or not, he was dependent on these experts. How he resented this dependency.

In a gentle and soothing voice, almost like his mother's, Zikron told Neal to sit in the waiting room. "Your wife is in good hands."

Neal wanted to believe this. He had to, so he stood up and gave Rita a kiss on her head. "I'll be right here when you finish, sweetheart," he said, leaving the room.

Before he reached the waiting room, Reet was screaming, "Don't you dare! Get away from me. How dare you!"

Now Irene: "It won't hurt. It's just a shot, Rita."

Neal walked to his chair and closed his eyes. Someone closed the hallway door. When he opened his eyes it was a quarter after five. He had left Rita with Zikron at four thirty and was surprised it was taking so long, but he also felt relieved. He pictured Rita being her happy old self when she walked through the door. He picked up the morning paper and started reading.

> Unconfined by Stadium walls and with
> Lake Erie as a backdrop, the gigantic show
> illuminated the skies for miles as ear-
> shattering explosions saluted the birth of a
> nation that stands as the bulwark of
> freedom in a world beset by aggression . . .

It killed him that his family had missed the July Fourth fireworks.

Neal threw the newspaper on the floor and remembered the folded papers in his pocket. He took them out, unfolded them, and began to read.

> 1. Patients must always be accompanied by the accompanying adult.
>
> 2. Since vomiting must be avoided at all costs, no food should be eaten by the patients for at least four hours before treatment.

Neal counted the hours since lunch and then remembered that Rita had not wanted to eat at all that day.

> 3. Patients should wear ordinary clothes, loosened around the waist; jacket and vest should be removed and shirt opened at the neck. Women: tight girdles should be removed.

4. Patients must empty bladder and remove false teeth before entering the treatment room.

5. Treatment is given on a hard padded couch with the patient lying on his back. A pad is placed beneath the dorsal vertebrae and a small pillow is placed under the head. Control of the patient's movements is essential during the fit (convulsion), if fractures are to be avoided. The patient is either held down by a trained staff of five nurses or covered by a special canvas restraining sheet (straitjacket) that the nurses hold down.

Neal swallowed. He felt ill. It sounded more like torture than treatment.

6. The nurse standing at the head cleans the forehead of the patient with saline. Electrodes, enclosed in lint pads, are then placed in position by the officiating doctor and maintained by a two-inch rubber band around the head.

7. A gag is inserted into the patient's mouth and the patient is asked to bite down hard. The mouth gag is held in place with the patient's chin firmly up

on the gag so that the jaw of the patient cannot open too far in the initial stage of the fit and risk a dislocation.

8. When everyone is in position, a switch is pressed.

9. Please note: There is no scientific evidence that variation of the current used is of any therapeutic value, provided it is enough to fire off a fit.

Who needed Korea? Fireworks? He had sent his poor helpless wife into the hands of trained men and women with degrees and permission to . . .

10. Movements are controlled. The most important part of this control is taking the strain of the initial jerk on the back to prevent flexion.

11. If breathing does not resume after the fit, a face mask delivering oxygen is provided.

Breathing not resume? These bastards might kill her!

12. Generally, after an hour or more, the patient is able to get up and go home. He should go to bed and be kept under supervision for the rest of the day. Often, there is a good deal of headache. The patient will be subdued

and quiet. There will be memory loss for several hours, but by the end of the cycle (6–12 treatments), partial memory returns.

13. Although the patient will be able to perform tasks, family members may notice a flatness of affect.

14. Remember! ECT erases the reaction to the traumatic event (stimulus) but does not erase the event itself.

Hands shaking, Neal tore the paper into small pieces and threw them into the waste basket next to the cuckoo clock. At quarter to six the door from the inner hallway opened and Irene Blackwell appeared, one arm around Rita's waist and the other holding her arm. His wife looked like the girls' Raggedy Ann doll, but her face lacked all expression. A soft moan emerged from somewhere in her body. Neal had never seen anyone with shell shock, but he imagined this was what they must look like. Irene sat Rita down in the velvet chair. She placed Rita's arms on the arm rests. Rita didn't rub her fingers on the velvet, like she had done before. In fact, she didn't move.

Irene explained it would be a good idea to sit in the waiting room like this until seven, just to make sure "everything is all right."

All right? How could everything be all right? What the hell was this woman talking about? His wife was a zombie, a medically induced zombie.

While Neal watched Rita, who looked as though she were floating in and out of consciousness, he wondered how in the name of heaven he would get her home in this condition and, if he did, what he would do with her there.

The newspaper on the floor stared up at him, but offered no relief.

> Behind the Lines: Wounds, Hunger . . . This Side of War Is not in Korea Communiques . . . A railroad station, North Korea . . . The wounded are quiet in straw-littered boxcars, waiting for someone to move them to a hospital. But for some the pain and the broiling sun is too much. They roll their heads back and forth, mouths open, moaning. . . . With sneers the wounded watch the South Korean soldiers, lolling at dress parade on the platform, waiting for a train to the front.

> It is the knowing contempt which the great fraternity of wounded always hold for the healthy.

* * *

On Wednesday, January 10, 1951, in the middle of the cold and bloody twentieth century, at exactly 3:16 p.m., Rita Stonehill walked down the dark-green hallway from Joey's room to the kitchen, carrying the light-brown wicker basket. A blue baby blanket was folded neatly on top. Beneath the blanket, Joey slept. Neal was waiting for her, standing at the sink, looking out the window at the falling snow. Weather reports said it was snowing all over Northeast Ohio and into Pennsylvania. It was snowing in Erie, and snow was falling too in Buffalo, New York. Niagara Falls, the weather reports predicted, would freeze.

When Neal heard Rita's footsteps, he turned toward her. Her face was ashen, like gray snow, her eyes bloodshot. She walked carefully, barely breathing. He wanted to weep. They had discussed what they were about to do for weeks, ever since the cerebral palsy specialist from Boston had checked Joey at seventeen months and expressed little optimism about his prognosis. Joey would never see, hear, smile, or crawl. This was the Bostonian's prediction, and he was an expert.

The decision to send Joey to an institution had hovered over them like a dark cloud ever since his birth. Finally, they had decided. Freund assured them that Woody Haven was the best facility in Northeast Ohio. Neal would take him there today, before the girls came home from school. The dark cloud was supposedly lifting, but Neal felt no relief, and from the looks of her, neither did Rita.

Neal wore his long winter coat and thick leather gloves. All he had to do was put on his hat and wrap his plaid wool scarf around his neck. Rita lifted the basket toward him, as if making an offering. *Here is my grief,* she could have said, but she said nothing.

"Do you want to kiss him goodbye?" Neal said.

She nodded. Looking at his sweet face in the basket, she bent down and placed a kiss on his cheek. "He's sleeping so peacefully."

Neal knew they would never forget this moment: the fridge buzzing behind them, the snow falling outside the window above the sink, Joey in the wicker laundry basket between them, asleep.

Neal tightened his scarf. "I'll be home by seven thirty, honey. Don't wait for me for dinner." He kissed her forehead and grasped the wicker basket with both hands. He didn't move until he was sure he had a firm and steady grip on each side. Thank goodness for the special medication for special babies the special Boston doctor had sent them. Hopefully, Joey would sleep for the two- to three-hour drive to Akron.

Rita put a finger on the edge of the wicker basket. Neal thought she wanted to keep holding on, but she just tucked the blanket under Joey's chin. Christ, he was a handsome little boy. Poor thing. Rita's hand moved with a delicacy and grace, the way she used to arrange cupcakes. Once he had called her "my cupcake . . ."

Neal carried the basket carefully down the back stairs. This was the easy part. What he couldn't figure out was why this had happened to him and Rita, and if they had really exhausted all their options. What if they had moved to New York or Boston? Maybe Joey would have come out of his vegetable state. Rita wouldn't hear of it, of course. She wasn't leaving Cleveland. This was her birthplace, where she grew up, where her mother and sister lived, and where her beloved father died and was buried.

What if they had held him all day long, like some crazy specialist suggested, not just the ten minutes here and there? What if they had hired a private physiotherapist to work with Joey every day and not just twice a week for thirty minutes? Could they have saved him from going to some godforsaken institution—"home" as they called it—in Akron? The *ifs* twisted his insides until he ached.

Outside, the cold bit into Neal's face and the small open space on his neck above his scarf. Icicles hung on the garage door. How would he get the damn door up without putting the wicker basket on the icy driveway? He bent down, gently, balancing the basket on his knees, holding it with one gloved hand while he used the other to jiggle and lift the garage door. He slid the basket onto the drier floor of the garage, then stood up to open the door all the way. Neal unlocked the yellow Chrysler, picked up the basket, its handles now cold, and slid it onto the back seat. Joey didn't make a peep.

What if the experts had offered to use experimental drugs on Joey?

He had to stop thinking like this. They had made a decision. Even the rabbi had given his blessing and told him (after Rita was out of earshot) that they should have another baby immediately. The whole goddamned thing broke his heart, but he was grateful Reet had bounced back. A miracle. After the eighth treatment with Zikron she awoke from a nap, complaining of a mild headache, like she had done after all the previous treatments. But this time she wanted to see Joey and the girls. She even wanted to cook dinner and watch television. It was as if the whole year before that moment had happened to someone else. His Reet was back, though she had no memory of what had happened from the day they brought Joey home from the hospital in October 1949 to the day she started to function again in September 1950. She ate. She mothered. She even responded to Neal's touch. Freund, the son of a bitch, had been right, and Zikron turned out to be a mensch, encouraging Neal after each treatment, despite the hardships.

Neal turned the key in the ignition. While he waited for the car to warm up, he lowered his head to the steering wheel. How could he do this? Deliver his only son, for whom he had waited forty-six years, to an institution, as if he were a basket of laundry?

He put the gearshift into reverse and maneuvered the icy driveway. Motor running, he jumped out to lower the garage door and then jumped back into the car. At the bottom of the driveway he stopped and looked down the street toward Buckeye Road. There were his two little girls walking home from school. Elizabeth was seven and a half, in second grade, and the little one was already five and a half, in kindergarten. How the time had flown by. Lately, the little one had stopped asking him for a story she could share at show-and-tell. They were sweet little girls, the way they walked home together holding hands and looking at the sidewalk, scanning with their sweet eyes for cracks below the ice. "Step on a crack, you break your mother's back," or something silly like that, they'd chant at home. He drove in their direction, hoping they wouldn't notice the family car. Later, would they notice Joey was gone?

At the stop sign on the corner of Ludlow and Buckeye, he stopped, lit a Camel, and turned on the radio. Bing Crosby sang "Dear Hearts and Gentle People." Neal hummed along.

* * *

Six weeks later, on a bitterly cold Saturday night, Neal was trying to read the paper while his two little girls laughed at a new comedian on *Cavalcade of Stars*. Rather than yell at the girls to stop laughing, like he usually did, on this night he put down the paper and watched with them. After a couple minutes he called to Rita in the kitchen, to come out and see the new comic.

"His name is Gleason, honey. Jackie Gleason. Plays an old-time bartender."

Rita called back from the kitchen to turn it down. Then the phone rang. The black kitchen phone rang. At 8:25 p.m. on Saturday night, February 24, 1951. Snow had been falling all day. It was a bad storm; the girls wouldn't be able to go to Sunday school in the morning. They'd probably be happy about that.

"It's for you, honey," Rita yelled from the kitchen. Reluctantly, he left Gleason before the punch line.

"Didn't get the name," Rita whispered as she handed him the receiver.

"Hello. Mr. Stonehill? This is Leah. I'm the home matron over here at Woody Haven."

"Woody Haven?" Was that a golf course or a funeral parlor for termites?

"The one in Akron. You know. We have your son, that is . . ."

Neal wanted to watch Jackie Gleason. Now some lady was pulling him back.

"Mr. Stonehill, I'm afraid there is no easy way to tell you this . . ."

"Could you please speak up, Lori? The mixer is going here."

"Leah."

"Okay. Leah."

"I said there is no easy way to tell you this."

Neal hated pussyfooting. He wanted to lick the bowl before Rita put it in the sink.

"I'm afraid——"

"Please speak up, Miss Leah. There's a mixer going here and Gleason is on TV."

"I'm afraid your son Joseph— no, I mean George Joseph— no, I see here Joey, yes . . . Joey on the form. Your son, sir, contracted pneumonia last week. I think you were notified, weren't you?"

Neal listened but said nothing. Of course he had been notified. He had even visited the little fella when he went down to Orrville on business, a short drive from Akron, but he hadn't told Rita. Why bother, when she was showing more signs of recovery every day, smiling, laughing, wanting to go learn the rumba with Evy and Mort, knitting Neal a sweater, even joining the PTA.

"I'm terribly sorry——"

"What?"

"He died this morning."

Neal's mouth fell open. He felt like someone had thrown a hardball into his chest. He collapsed onto the closest kitchen chair and told Rita, without looking at her, to turn off the mixer, but she didn't hear. He had been expecting the call every day ever since he had left Joey at Woody Haven, but still, the reality of it was shocking.

"Could you repeat that, miss?"

"I said that your son Joey died this morning, Mr. Stonehill. I'm terribly sorry."

Neal looked at Rita. She was holding the spatula above the bowl that was flying in circles. Or was that his head going in circles? Alive, dead, today, yesterday, baby boy, vegetable, dead, alive. Rita lifted the spatula as if it were the torch on the Statue of Liberty. Was this good news or bad?

She lowered her arm and turned off the mixer. The silence jolted Neal, one more punch. "Yes, yes," he said into the receiver, closing his eyes for a second. When he opened them, Reet was wiping the beaters clean. She rolled the dough and started making the heart-shaped cookies and placing them delicately on a cookie sheet. Surrounded by fresh dough, hearts, and the smell of vanilla, Rita looked glamorous in her gray apron with the yellow forsythias.

Only two days ago they had talked about filling in the forms for a country club. Neal had even succeeded in broaching the subject of having another baby, and for the first time, Rita listened.

Of course he knew it was coming. Didn't everyone say that special babies don't live long? But so soon? Was this more foul play? He couldn't figure it out.

"Are you there, Mr. Stonehill?" came the voice on the other end of the line.

"Yes, I'm here." His shaky voice surprised him. He was almost squeaking, like Joey.

"The poor thing died at six fifteen this morning," she said. "The body is here if you want to come down . . . I know it's stormy out now, Mr. Stonehill. I know you folks have been through a lot."

Neal wondered what she knew. He and Rita were trying to forget the past and here was this woman acknowledging for the first time that they *had* been through a lot. He wanted to hang up on her and hold on at the same time.

"Perhaps it's all for the best in cases like this," she said. "How can we help you?"

Was she reading a script? Was this the way all parents were notified that their special babies had died at Woody Haven? Neal almost pitied her.

Rita slid the cookie sheet into the oven with what seemed like an enormous effort. She closed the oven door, wiped her hands on the towel next to the sink, and left the kitchen without looking at him.

"No, we don't need any help," Neal said, collecting himself to sit up straight. "These things happen. For you, probably, all the time."

Neal hung up the phone. He stood still, placed both hands on the counter, and lowered his head. He wanted to pray—words, a song, anything—but he didn't have the words, so he walked through the dark hallway to their bedroom.

Rita was lying on her stomach across the bedspread, her head buried in her pillow. He stood in the doorway and shut the door behind him.

"We did everything we could, sweetheart," he said, with what he felt was love.

She shook her head. He didn't know if she was agreeing or not. He sat on the edge of the bed. Her back was long and graceful. He wanted to touch her but was afraid she might wince. Outside the window facing Ludlow Road, snow fell, incessant and silent, as if it would never stop and they would all be buried, like Joey, in a white blanket of cold.

"How do we tell the girls?" Neal asked, after a few moments of deathly silence.

Rita said nothing.

"Maybe I'll call Freund. Or Zikron."

Rita sniffled, cleared her throat, and said in a faint voice, "Call the rabbi."

Neal walked back to the living room. The credits were being displayed on the TV screen.

"It was so funny," Elizabeth said.

Neal lit up a Camel and inhaled all the way to his crotch.

"Jackie Gleason was fighting with Alice because she spent all his money on a new dress."

"So?" Neal exhaled.

"So, Jackie Gleason said, 'To da moon, Alice. I'm gonna send ya straight to da moon.'"

Neal didn't laugh. The little one piped in, "As if people could go to the moon."

He picked up the newspaper. He wanted to remember the date—February 24, 1951.

THE HUMAN THING TO DO

What February Means

by Charles McCune

The old clock keeps a-turnin' and we keep a-hustlin' trying to cut our slice of fame and fortune when suddenly we pause to catch a breath and realize, it's February.

February! The month that's filled with great dates and names; the month we dare not pass unnoticed. The month of which we hear the praises sung to George and Abe and Tom; to the four chaplains who chanted prayers in different tongues as they plunged beneath the waves aboard the fighting Dorchester. It's the month in which we celebrate National Brotherhood Week. . . .

Here in a world of conflict and confusion, it is a great time for us to think of helping men toward a firmer bond of brotherhood. Brotherhood . . . is the avenue down which all of us should travel in our effort to make this a better world in which to live.

It's February! Remember what it means.

* * *

A month later Rita was lying on her chartreuse chaise in her pink negligee, whining that the beauty shop had ruined her hair with its new frosting concoction. She had just wanted highlights and Tony poured on the whole bottle. Neal told her to get over it. She still looked beautiful. She reached out for *Raising Your Children in the Modern Age*. Neal had bought it for her in December for her thirtieth birthday, two weeks before he had driven

Joey to Akron. He was glad Reet had started showing interest in the ins and outs of what they called child-rearing. In his day back in Iowa, it was just a one-handed slap on the bottom or a one-handed tussle of the hair. Rita would have none of that. Her father had always been loving, caring, and gentle with her. He taught her how to ice skate.

She turned to the chapter entitled "Family Crisis" and read to him. "Research at universities throughout the country now shows that disasters such as bankruptcy, rape or a death in the family should be shielded from the young child for as long as possible until the child's ego (see Glossary) is strong enough to cope with the disaster. If the disaster is health related, your pediatrician should be consulted before any discussion with younger children. If a death is experienced in the family, contact your clergy for further support."

"So that's what we're doing," she said, "right?"

"What, honey?" Neal was counting the small change that he kept in his underwear drawer.

"We're having our clergy come for support."

Neal reminded her that they had discussed it almost every night since the call. Rabbi Green was scheduled to come tomorrow to tell the girls. He picked up the sports page.

"Do you think it's the best idea?" Rita sounded scared.

"What?"

"To have Rabbi Green tell them."

"I don't know, honey. I'm no expert. You just read me what it says in the book. Research and all. You just read it to me." Was she forgetting again? Neal had hoped Rabbi Green could have come to the house on the day of the cremation, but he was tied up. Rita had stayed home that day. There was no reason to make a big to-do, and who knew how she might have reacted.

"Rabbis know how to do this sort of thing," Neal told Rita. "Remember?"

When the doorbell rang the next day, Neal was sitting on the love seat in the living room reading the Sunday paper and Rita was in the kitchen preparing french toast and bacon. The beloved smell permeated their home. The little one ran down the stairs to open the heavy front door.

"So nice of you to come over, Rabbi," Neal said, taking the rabbi's coat and hat, wet with sleet. "I'll tell the missus you're here."

"That won't be necessary, Neal," said the rabbi. "I just want to talk to the girls."

The rabbi sat down in the middle of the living room couch, underneath the cheap watercolor Neal had picked up during his final trip to Iowa. He was glad he had chosen a farm scene, even though Rita thought it amateur. Neal told the little one to take her thumb out of her mouth and go find Elizabeth. "The rabbi wants to talk to you girls."

He went to stand near the door of their bedroom, straining to hear the rabbi's words. He heard the girls mumble something or other after the rabbi. Then the rabbi asked them where their wonderful father was, because he needed his coat.

Neal walked back into the living room. When the rabbi stood up, the little one started bawling, screaming, and crying hysterically and ran into the kitchen.

"Thanks, Rabbi, for coming over," Neal said, giving the rabbi his coat. "I'll send you a check."

The rabbi put a hand on Neal's shoulder and gave an understanding smile.

"It's over now," Neal said. "I'm awfully sorry about the little one . . . I guess she took it pretty hard."

Rabbi Green put on his heavy black coat. "She's a child, Neal. It's normal."

Neal accompanied the rabbi to the top of the stairs. As he watched Rabbi Green walk down, he felt a strange emptiness in his stomach. He moved back to stand against the wall, fearing he might fall. After the rabbi slammed the front door downstairs shut, Neal walked the few steps and stood in front of the door to their apartment. He clutched the doorknob with both hands and stood there for a few minutes to collect himself. He needed collecting, fearing he might collapse. He felt abandoned, alone with his family—Rita and the girls, no son, though Joey's room was still there, the crib still with a sheet and the frisky red farmyard animals still drifting across the wallpaper. Kind of like the way Joey had drifted through their lives. For the first time in years, Neal had no idea what he should do, what he *could* do or *must* do.

Suddenly, the words Rita had read the night before assaulted him: "crisis," "disaster," "death in the family." That had been his life, from June 18, 1949, until today. It had happened to *him*, not to some character in a book or stranger in the newspaper. To him, Neal Stonehill. Now, supposedly, the crisis was over, the disaster relegated to the past, the body gone.

But was it? As the slam of the front door echoed in the hallway, Neal thought about the only man who had stood by him at the cremation, the keeper of comforting words, Rabbi Green, who had walked back into the cold. Waves of guilt and fear, grief and remorse washed over him. The skin on his hands tingled and he felt dizzy. Was this mourning? Was he supposed to mourn? Had not the whole lousy past twenty months been one extended mourning? If not, how long would he feel this way? When would it end?

Joey's soul, whatever that was, still seemed to hover in the house, like a constant shadow, a presence there and not there, wafting in the dark hallway, clinging to the stucco walls. What had the rabbi said about goodness and mercy? They would follow him all the days of his life.

Would Joey too?

Neal turned the knob slowly and opened the door. He walked back into the room where his past and future collided. It was empty. The familiar smell of french toast and bacon, splattered with the little one's cries, lured him into the kitchen. He rushed to protect Reet.

Part Three: The Mourning After

...and the days of thy mourning shall be ended.

Isaiah 60:20

Chapter One: Giving

At a trendy restaurant on Emek Refaim Street—Valley of the Ghosts or Valley of the Giants, depending on the historical context—my mother nibbles at a wheat berry, black bean, and celery salad. Today's context is a mishmash of gigantic ghosts and ghostly giants. Yitzhak Rabin was assassinated last month, and I am mourning not only him but the whole Israeli peacemaking enterprise that no longer exists. Ever since 1982, when Israel invaded Lebanon and Elliot returned with symptoms of shell shock, the romantic dream of Israel that I swallowed whole at twenty-one has been fading year by year.

We're celebrating my mother's seventy-fifth birthday in a restaurant where everything—chairs, tables, floor, walls, plates, napkins, menus—is either pastel turquoise, pastel peach, or a mixture of both. This is trendy in the nineties. It's the same décor as the nursing home in Florida where my father died in 1992, drifting in and out of consciousness for three days while my mother searched for ways to absent herself from the moment of death. I flew to Sarasota from Israel to witness his death. "Want to go to McDonald's?" Mom asked me the last night of his life. No. I wanted to see my father's transition from giant to ghost.

As my mother sticks two fingers with polished nails into her mouth to dislodge a sliver of celery, I tell her I have Joey's death certificate and, before she can respond, I add, "I want you to have it."

What I don't tell her is that I want to step out of the past and shut the door, like those tourists across the street, who are shutting the green iron door to the Templar Cemetery behind them. It's time. Giving my mother the Certificate of Death may seem an untidy birthday gift, but I don't know where else it belongs.

"Your mother has class," my friends have been telling me for years, every time they see her at a bris or bar mitzvah. At seventy-five her frosted cropped hair frames her oval face like solid hands. An elegant peach-and-turquoise silk scarf wrapped with pizzazz around her neck holds her face aloft—a small pedestal supporting the head of a marble Demeter. December sunlight shines into the restaurant, illuminating her vibrant gray-green eyes, her own white teeth, and her smooth Hungarian skin. (My skin is White Russian wrinkles.) My mother carries herself with a strong, independent bearing, but I wonder, now, as I plan to give her this gift, if her strength covers a threatening fragility. Does the frailty my father used as a reason to protect her from the cries of her bereft children the day the rabbi came to the house, and forever after, lurk beneath?

"I wrote to Vital Statistics in Akron," I say, looking down at my tuna salad and then up again, trying to maintain a matter-of-fact stance. "After your letter, I needed more facts."

She listens, though her eyes focus on the italian parsley caught on the tip of her fork.

"For seven dollars they sent me . . . our past."

"What?" She drops the fork onto her plate. "Whose?"

I look again at the cemetery across the street. German Templars who came to Jerusalem in the nineteenth century are buried there, as well as other Christians who came later and "fell asleep in Jesus" or "passed to the New Jerusalem." The stones are engraved in a multiplicity of languages: Hebrew, Arabic, English, German, Dutch, Russian, Greek, and Chinese.

Perhaps this cemetery and not the décor is the reason I chose this particular restaurant. It helps me focus on my mission—giving back the grief. I do not want my body to be a vessel for Joey and my mother's sorrow for one more day. No longer will Joey live in my muscles, chest, and back, where his death and my grief solidified, causing that breathing tic on the inhale.

"Do you want it, Mom?" I ask, shocking us both.

The waitress walks by and smiles. My mother asks for water. "Why don't they bring it with the meal?" she asks me, even though she's visited Israel more than ten times and knows waitresses never serve water unless asked. "You haven't touched your salad, Judy. Don't you want to eat?"

I turn back to the green iron door. Despite the life-affirming Zionist experiment over the last one hundred–plus years, Jerusalem is still a city of the dead. For two thousand years, sick and old Jews came here to die, not live. Even today, dying Jews from abroad request they be buried in Jerusalem. Jerusalem is "the city besieged by [an] army of the dead," wrote Herman Melville in 1857. "Jerusalem is mournful and dreary and lifeless," wrote Mark Twain ten years later. "I would not desire to live here."

The City of Peace, as Jerusalem is sometimes translated, actually refers to the city of *eternal* peace. This is the Jerusalem that pulled me in when I was twenty-one. Jerusalem calls to those in search of the past. From the oldest Jewish cemetery in the world on the Mount of Olives in the east to the far newer Jewish cemetery in Givat Shaul in the west, from the tombs of King David and the Prophet Samuel on the hills to the Catholic and Protestant tombs of Jesus in the center, and in the center of the center, where an ancient stone wall is watered with tears, its chinks filled with handwritten notes to God, Jerusalem's stones embody national and religious longing and grief. *Come back*, the city calls. *Remember. Mourn.*

I know my mother does not want to hear this version. She prefers the internationally famous Israel Museum, high-end ethnic galabiyas at Maskit, and folk-dancing performances for tourists. She wants water and a toothpick. With a flimsy napkin she dabs the corners of her lips, takes her mirror and lipstick from her purse, and applies Spring Peach. I pay the bill.

"We're going to your writing room now?" she asks, a certain reticence in her voice.

"Yes," I say, with forced assertion, as doubts begin to rise within. We walk out of the restaurant, my mother ahead of me. I catch up to her and we head north on Valley of the Ghosts. My mother walks with a youthful bounce. I walk slower, lugging our pasts. She marvels at all the jewelry stores on the street. Maybe I should be giving her opals or pearls.

At the end of the street, across from the gas station, before we turn right, she asks about the hill in the distance across the Valley of Hinnom.

"That's Mount Zion," I say, looking at the iconic hill, "as in," and now I stop walking to sing, in a pseudo-operatic voice, Cantor Bushman's rendition of the verses from Isaiah:

> Come ye and let us go up to the mountain
> of the Lord,
>
> Unto the House of the God of Jacob.
>
> And He will teach us of his ways.
>
> And we will walk in His paths,
>
> for out of Zion shall go forth the Law
>
> and the Word of the Lord from Jerusalem.

"Oh, my," she says. "You remember all that? Doesn't look like much from here."

"The song and the place moved me once," I say.

We start to walk again.

"How much longer do we have?"

We pass the railroad station that, since 1892, has connected Jerusalem to the rest of the world. We turn right onto Hebron Road and then left, up an alley into the neighborhood of Abu Tor, Father of the Bull. My writing room is in Abu Tor, one of three rooms in a shared rental of a basement apartment on Nachshon Street. In the Jewish oral tradition, during the Exodus from Egypt, Nachshon was the first Israelite to wade into the water of the Red Sea. He forged ahead until the water reached his nose. Only then did God split the sea for the Children of Israel.

I used to admire and want that kind of faith, Nachshon faith, but not anymore. Sorrow is reaching my nostrils and I'm tired. All I want now is freedom from mourning and compulsive retrospection. All this I do not tell my mother.

"I hope you have a bathroom," she says.

We enter my stark white room. At one end is a white table the length of the white wall, at the other end a new Simmons Hide-a-Bed, off-white. On the floor is a new white carpet, low pile. The design impulse came from Florida. I wanted to feel close to my mother, who lives in Sarasota amid manicured lawns, magnolias, and crotons, where neighborhoods of peach-colored one-story houses carry names like Crystal Lakes and Palm Aire; where the old go, not to remember and die, but to golf, swim, and enjoy the good life in posh rooms with white carpets, white leather chairs, and white ceilings that reach toward heaven.

As we stand together in my sparse white room, afternoon light strains to penetrate dirty gray windows at the top of the far wall and I do not feel close to my mother.

She goes to the bathroom while I look at the Joey file. It bulges from white binders that stand like sentinels along the table.

"How do you flush?" she asks when she returns, walking toward the Hide-a-Bed. She sits down. I go flush for her, come back, and stand next to the binders. "Nice fabric," she says, rubbing the white polyester-and-wool armrest. Her left hand moves in small counterclockwise circles, and her right hand rubs the cushion next to her in clockwise circles. Is she treading water? Drowning? Or is she hoping, with all this rubbing, to feel something new?

I remember rubbing her red chinchilla coat on a winter afternoon. Maybe it was January 1951, while Joey lived in Akron, when I was five and a half and in kindergarten at Ludlow School, or late February, after Joey died. Maybe it was January 1952, after Jim was born and I was in first grade learning to read and write, and maybe the when doesn't matter. All that matters is, together, we shoveled snow, clearing the deep white cold from the front door on Ludlow and the path that led to the rest of the world. With longing I remember that day—the searing clean snow, the red scottish-plaid scarf wrapped tightly around her neck, her brown leather gloves, the strength with which she held the shovel, the ease with which she threw the snow to the sides, her not looking at me, as I, holding my toy shovel, stared at her, wanting to be like her, to be held by her, to feel close to her, to be her.

What is she thinking now as she rubs my white couch?

If I had rubbed her red chinchilla coat long and hard, would I have been able to touch her?

"Nice fabric," she repeats. "How much did you pay?"

I pour out the Joey papers onto the desk as an archaeologist reveals her gems. These scrambled papers are my genizah. Here is the letter from Rabbi Green and the form from Billow's Funeral Homes and Crematory. Here is my mother's letter on yellow legal pad paper. (Can this distant woman sitting on my couch be the same one who penned that warm, open letter?) Here are the photocopies of microfiche pages from the *Cleveland Plain Dealer* from 1949, 1950, and 1951, the cover of the Lowell sheet music of "Joey," my notebooks filled with writings and rewritings of memories, fictions, and what ifs, drafts and rewrites of drafts, as well as earlier versions of this book, the writings which have kept me afloat for decades.

On the back of an envelope is the last verse from Adrienne Rich's "Diving into the Wreck," written with a red ballpoint pen.

> We are, I am, you are
> by cowardice or courage
> the one who find our way
> back to this scene
> carrying a knife, a camera
> a book of myths
> in which
> our names do not appear.

And here is a quote from Albert Camus, scrawled on the back of an invitation to a bar mitzvah:

> A man's work is nothing but this slow trek
> to rediscover, through the detours of art,

> those two or three great and simple images
> in whose presence his heart first opened.

"Or closed," I wrote underneath, with a question mark.

"What are you looking for?" my mother asks, opening and closing her purse.

"The Certificate of Death," I say. "I want to give it to you."

"Well . . . if you think so," she says, looking at her watch.

Nine months to the week after Joey died, my mother gave birth to James Neal, a healthy blond baby who, like the biblical Joseph, saved the family. Grandma was in place in the upstairs bedroom. Vashti the maid came four times a week to clean floors and mangle sheets. Mother and Father now had the time, energy, and mental health to learn the rumba and cha-cha, to bowl and golf, to vacation in Puerto Rico, St. Thomas, Mexico, and the Virgin Islands. My mother brought me dolls from each country. They sat on a glass shelf in a shadow box over my bed. These were the angels who protected me from above while my mother played mah-jongg, canasta, and bridge.

Once Jim was born we became the iconic 1950s Midwest American family: Father worked hard and earned well; Mother became president of the PTA; the well-behaved little girls learned plié and piano; the little boy learned to bat. We ate dinners together, and when we spoke, we spoke only in present and future tense.

Here is Joey's Certificate of Death, a piece of A4. I read it for the last time. Now I am good at reading it, no gulping the way people do to suppress uncomfortable feelings. I no longer read *into* the text. Once it held the power of a magic scroll. Now, two months short of forty-four years after Joey's death, the certificate reverts to its initial status—a bureaucratic form. Every detail, even the category for survivors, where my name does not appear, is dry text, though stained with tears. Holding it in my hand, I turn toward my mother, who is now kneeling on the white rug and rubbing its pile. I kneel opposite her, hand steady, telling myself it is okay to give my mother her son's death certificate.

"Here it is, Mom," I say. I hold it out to her as one might make an offering to a goddess—or demon— begging for appeasement and calm.

She takes it with one hand and says, "Nice rug," as she slowly pushes herself up with her empty hand. Standing, she looks at the form, trying to focus on the small print. She could take out her reading glasses from her purse but chooses not to. She squints at the paper as if it might be a shard from a foreign land. The word of the Lord from Jerusalem? A relic from the time the Lord reigned from Mount Zion? Her eyes ask, *How did this get here?* The fingers of her right hand rub the paper, front and back, back and forth, and I wonder, Is the purpose of all this rubbing to access feeling? Does she *not* feel?

Or—and the idea astounds me—to erase? If so, what? The past? Her feelings? Memories?

I cannot read my mother.

Suddenly I am overcome with sadness and guilt. The gift seems a cruel offering.

My mother moves to the couch, sits down, and folds the paper into her purse. In a voice barely audible, she says, "We never had a photo . . ."

I stand and look into her damp eyes and feel compassion. I move to kneel at her feet. I want her to put her hands on my head and bless me, and at the same time I want to hold her in my arms, rub her head, and bless her. *There, there, sweetheart. Everything will be all right,* we could say to each other.

I walk toward my desk and then turn toward her again. She is standing now, walking toward me, asking what percentage of the rug is wool. As we meet in the center of the room, she is no longer a giant and I a little girl looking up. She is neither goddess nor demon. She is simply a mother and daughter, as I am, and we are the same height.

"I bought candlesticks," she whispers, looking toward the gray window.

Chapter Two: Reading and Writing

This time I drive up Mount Zion in my own car. There's a parking lot near King David's Harp, an event hall for life cycle parties. During the thirty years between my first visit to Mount Zion and today's, the mountain has enjoyed serious facelifts to accommodate the thousands of tourists visiting the supposed sites of King David's burial and Jesus's last supper. The parking lot boasts a parade of shiny tour buses. Mount Zion, the hillside no higher than a beginner's ski slope in eastern Ohio, where most of the property is owned by the Diaspora Yeshiva, now bustles with action. American men in their early twenties flock to the yeshiva in search of their Judaism.

On this particular spring day, I am in search of the names I couldn't read in 1966, the names of dead children of whose history I was ignorant, toward whom I felt a paralyzing guilt, and because of whom I researched and resurrected the story of my own dead brother. But as soon as I start walking on the stone paths of Mount Zion, I feel uneasy, for there is no sign for the Cave of Remembrance. There is, however, an enormous Crusader building with a sign pointing to its basement dungeon that reads "Chamber of the Holocaust."

Nothing looks familiar. The guard at the entrance requests a small fee. "For upkeep," he says. I hand him a ten-shekel coin that he drops into a plastic cup.

I walk down a few stone stairs into a sprawl of six connecting cavernous rooms with dim electric lighting. In one, plaques in Hebrew *and* English cover the walls with names of European communities destroyed during World War II. I try to read some of the names: Bielica, Tokaj, Nyírbátor, Pestszenterzsébet. They mean nothing to me, though I'm sure they mean a lot to the descendants of loved ones who lived and died in those hard-to-pronounce places. Off this cave is another one with row upon row of what looks like post office mailboxes. On each box is an electric candle. There are names on the mailbox plaques in Hebrew and English: Fajwel Szental, Zoltan Lefkovits, Yitzhak Mitler, Berek Szenkman, Tema and Haskel Lehrer, Jeremiah Shmaltzer, Ruchel Blumenstyk, each name a world destroyed. After Jozi-

Herman Markovits, I understand I am looking for a particular name that does not appear because it does not belong here.

On my way out of the Chamber of the Holocaust, a sign hanging from the ceiling near the exit attracts my attention: "Your brother's blood cries out to Me from the ground. *Genesis 4:10.*"

These are God's words to Cain after Cain murdered his brother Abel and tried to relinquish responsibility by asking, "Am I my brother's keeper?"

Yes, I am my brother's keeper. I have kept his name alive for decades, and now I want him to rest.

I once read in an anthropology book that civilizations began when people started to bury their dead.

At the exit I stop to speak with the guard. He is reading Psalms. Something is pulling me to stay in this cave. I am not yet ready to leave Mount Zion. The guard asks if I saw the jacket made from Torah parchments, sewn by a Jew. Before I can reply he tells me it was worn by a Nazi to a fancy ball. "He wanted to humiliate the Jews," he tells me. "But the Jew who sewed it was very clever. He took the parchments from the portion in Deuteronomy Ki Tavo, where are listed many curses of evildoing. So this big-shot Nazi was wearing a jacket from the Torah, but that jacket screamed in silence that the Nazi himself was evil and wicked. You understand?"

Yes, I told him and explained I was more interested in the names than the artifacts. "I visited this place in 1966, but it was very different."

"Of course. It was run down then," he said, keeping one finger in his book. "Only mourners came. Anybody who wanted to learn about the Holocaust went to Yad v'Shem over on Mount Herzl." He lifted his chin in the direction of Mount Herzl.

"What do you mean 'only mourners'?" I asked.

"You know. Survivors. People who lost family in Europe and had no place to mourn. They came here. They still come. To the cave . . ."

"The Cave of Remembrance?"

"Yes," he said. "That's what they called it then. The Cave of Remembrance. They come and say kaddish and light candles and cry. Once in '49 or '50 some of the survivors they brought ashes from a concentration camp over there in Europe. Can you believe? I don't remember which one. Nobody knew whose ashes they were, so everyone can think it's his brother or her sister or mother, father."

I feel dizzy and look for a chair to sit down, but there is none.

"Now we have a cur-a-tor," he says, as if it is a pretentious word. "You know what that is?"

I nod but cannot absorb more. Abruptly, I turn to leave. "Thank you. Thank you so much, sir," I say looking back. "Thank you."

"Come back," he says, returning to his Psalms.

* * *

My Joey is one of a long tradition of dead brothers rising. He is not the first to be resurrected from a dungeon in order to save, but he is the first for me. There was the biblical Joseph, the brother whose absence proved a strong presence and who came back to save not only his family but also the Children of Israel.

"*Hineni!*" I say to the tour bus drivers sitting together in the baggage area of a bus, sipping Turkish coffee. "Behold, I am here!" I say to the young man selling warm Jerusalem bagels from a cart. "*Hineni!*" I say to some yeshiva students walking by. Nobody acknowledges me, so used are Jerusalemites to people losing . . . and finding themselves in Jerusalem.

On the short drive home I think about the years I struggled with learning Hebrew. Hebrew forces the reader and speaker to master roots. In the kiln of verbal alchemy, all Hebrew words are constructed from three-letter roots. The root of silence (*shtika*) is *shin, taf, kuf,* and the root of paralysis (*shituk*) is also *shin, taf, kuf.* In Hebrew my personal history congealed: the paralyzed baby—*mshutak*—and the silenced mother—*mshuteket.* Everything connects underneath in the fertile soil of our collective unconscious, all roots feeding each other in our shared history.

This is the natural place to end, but I cannot end. Ever since Joey disappeared without any goodbyes, the difficulty of saying goodbye is embossed on my psyche like the mole on the inside of my left arm. That is why my work at Neot Kedumim, the Biblical Landscape Reserve, is so satisfying. I guide pilgrims. They come to me for an hour or two and then they leave, off to the ruins of Gezer or Caesarea, all separations prescheduled.

My pilgrims at Neot Kedumim are interested in the real settings of the mythic stories from the Holy Land. They believe that if they can see, smell, and touch the settings, then the stories are true. In the "pilgrymage of the soul," coined by William Caxton in the fifteenth century, rather than travel east or west, north or south, the soul pilgrims dive deep into their personal stories. The sacred center, rather than being a piece of contested geography, becomes the heart of one's story, a rare weave of fact and fiction, a cradle of intermingling fibers that hold and rock the soul between comfort and tolerable discomfort.

During this back and forth, there is a constant series of rebirths and returnings. The return is always to the here and now, each time with more fervor and awareness, eyes wider, feet more firmly planted on earth. Whereas the route of the pilgrimage to the Holy Land may be marked with lines on a map, that of the soul is marked with tears, smiles, and wrinkles.

Wait. One last thought about God. If God was my guide who spoke to me in the Cave of Remembrance and guided my journey—a question always on my mind—then he spoke in a long continuous hush. I needed to listen every day, to pay attention for decades, in order to understand. Deuteronomy 30:14 comes to mind:

> The word is very near to you,
> In your mouth and in your heart
> To do it.

I want to do it. Now. I want to say, "That's all, folks!" and go buy a falafel.

I want to put Joey to rest and am getting closer. But I'm not finished yet. I want to reach that point where "we beat on, boats against the current, borne back ceaselessly into the past," only to return to the present, empowered.

I arrive home, and as I open the car door, I remember that I have never seen Joey's Certification of Birth. I slam the door. How could I have forgotten such an important document? Here we go again. I rush upstairs and write to the Bureau of Vital Statistics in Cleveland's Department of Public Health and enclose a check for twenty-five dollars, as instructed.

While I wait for a reply, I collect all my Joey papers into two Coke cartons. I say goodbye to each page, envelope, and scrap. I close the cartons securely with strong, wide tape and attach the following letter to a Mrs. Tzelophchat in the Ministry of the Interior, Jaffa Road, downtown Jerusalem:

Dear Mrs. Tzelophchat,

My brother George Joseph was born a vegetable on June 18, 1949, in Cleveland, Ohio, and as much as I wanted him to stay alive, he died on February 24, 1951. The place of his ashes is unknown. As a tikkun, I am asking you to bury these papers on the Mount of Olives. Please place the texts in a basket woven from the fibers of date palms. Below the Dead Sea Scrolls in the Shrine of the Book, I once saw a glass plate that had been perfectly preserved since 135 CE. The plate had been found in a cave near Jericho, wrapped in such a basket.

Near the burial site on the Mount of Olives, please attach the following sign:

George Joseph Stonehill

June 18, 1949, Cleveland, Ohio

February 24, 1951, Akron, Ohio

GONE HOME

I happened upon "Gone Home" when I roamed through a cemetery in Quaker City, Ohio, in 1965. I drove down there by myself on a summer day to attend a folk festival, but it turned out to be an old folks' festival, so I moseyed over to the local cemetery on a hill, and a little girl was there, five or six years old, skipping from gravestone to gravestone, as if playing hopscotch. I was struck by her ease and nonchalance, as well as by the profound simplicity of those two words: "Gone Home." Death felt so light in the middle of a summer day in that cemetery.

I appreciate how weird this request may sound, Mrs. Tzelophchat, but who if not you can understand the need for a place to mourn. I realize you deal only with genizahs and I am aware this is no genizah, but the name of God *does* appear at least once and, if God is truth, then more than once. Please let me know how much all this costs and I will send a check immediately.

With gratitude,

With compassion for all those who grieve,

With compassion for all those who can't say goodbye,

I am eternally yours,

Most sincerely,

Hineni

Chapter Three: Leaving

Pilgrims and tourists come from all over the world to visit Neot Kedumim, the man-made 635-acre nature reserve, where the trees, flowers, and shrubs mentioned in Jewish and Christian biblical texts flourish. In this unique place, the biblical past comes to life as I lead my charges down ancient cisterns, where we imagine Joseph's plight. Above the cistern, we reenact the love scene between Jacob and Rachel. We sit under tall date palms on the top of a hill to commune with the prophetess Deborah. In the shade of the Middle East sycamore tree we read Amos. In Byzantine winepresses we stomp on real grapes, and at a Roman olive press we nudge the donkey that pushes the beam that holds the stone that crushes the olives that breaks the pits that get pressed to extract the olive oil.

Busloads of tourists and pilgrims applaud me daily. My colleagues adore me for developing family celebrations— a *b'nai mitzvah* treasure hunt, a *b'nai mitzvah* vineyard, and biblical shtick for adults. I am the queen of Bible Lite and my self-esteem has soared. Working at this man-made nature reserve is the closest to working in the Garden of Eden, pre-guilt.

Now, in March of 1998, I have been dirtying my hands with visitors from around the world—Jews, Christians, and Hindus, young and old, believers and atheists—by making mud bricks six to twelve times a week. We dirty our hands in a batter of straw, water, and mud while imagining, with my encouragement, Egyptian slavery. After Brick Building 101, I lead each group to a shaded overlook with a table covered with branches of hyssop. From the lookout, the tourists see the modest gray-green hyssop bushes hugging the surrounding gray limestone rocks. "Take a sprig of hyssop," I say, quoting Moses in chapter twelve, verse twenty-two, of the Book of Exodus, "and dip it in the blood that is in the basin."

Each tourist picks up a sprig of hyssop, takes it to a table, and dips it in the plastic cup filled with red food coloring.

"Take the hyssop and touch the lintel and the two side posts of your door," I continue, and ask them to paint the wooden post of the lookout with the hyssop's fuzzy little absorbent gray-green leaves. Thus, hundreds, if not thousands, of visitors at Neot Kedumim relive the night God, dressed as the Angel of Death, passed over the houses of the Children of Israel during His mission to smite only the Egyptians. I enjoy this hands-on activity that makes the experience of leaving Egyptian slavery come to life. Doing it six times a week fills me with a strong sense of agency.

A month later, on the night of deliverance itself, my family is celebrating Passover at home with close friends and family. The smell of homemade chicken soup fills the house with memories of my Hungarian grandmother and her hard knaidlach. (Mine are soft, made from an Osem mix.) Miriam helped me make the charoset yesterday, using my mother's recipe. Just as the apple, walnut, and sweet wine concoction symbolizes the mortar that bound the bricks made by the Israelite slaves, so three thousand two hundred years later our charoset binds one generation to the next.

The tablecloth is white and so is Elliot's shirt. After twenty-six years of marriage, he is still as handsome as that Anglo-Israeli I fell in love with when we were both new immigrants, trying to figure out how and where we belonged in Jerusalem's mosaic. Our children have survived the Israeli secular education system, and we share none of their memories, being strangers in a strange but beloved land. We are still like our grandparents:

immigrants. Tonight I look forward to Elliot leading the seder. His singing voice is still loud and melodious, and his Hebrew never betrays his Canadian roots. He sits at one end of the oblong folding table and I sit opposite him, close to the kitchen. His kiddush does not disappoint.

After the kiddush, he asks everyone to stand up and place one hand on the seder plate. At the count of three, eleven Jews raise the seder plate over the middle of the table as though it were a large parchment. While elevating it, the plate elevates us into the realm of mythic meal. Together we sing the words of the ritual text: Ha Lachma, Behold the Matza. "This is the bread our ancestors ate as slaves in Egypt. In the past we were slaves, next year we will be free." Elliot tells us when and how to lower the plate, and we sit down.

Reading through the Haggadah, the book full of tales that Jews have used to remind generations of the Exodus from Egypt, the book in which Moshe's name does not appear, Elliot suggests we sing together the four questions. The four questions are actually one—Why is this night different from all other nights?—with four different answers. By the end of the fourth answer, despite my loving feeling for the people around the table and my delight that we as a family are hosting a seder, another question intrudes: Why do I stay with my in-house Pharaoh?

* * *

For years I have been writing a story in my head called "Pine." In the story Elliot and I get into the family car, he commanding the driver's seat and me passively traveling in the passenger seat. We are going for a hike in the woods. After thirty minutes of driving in silence he turns off the motor, stopping the car before we reach the trail. "Get out," he says, and I do. Then he gets out and starts walking toward the trail. I follow him. He turns around and asks me why I am following him.

"I thought we were taking a walk together," I say.

"Suit yourself," he says, and continues walking ahead of me. We walk on the trail for ten minutes in silence until we come to a clearing and he says, "Stand against that pine tree, your back to the tree." I do as I'm told, believing that one day he will love me if I obey. He walks away, then turns around to face me. This is the beginning of the story I have been afraid to transcribe.

After the four questions Elliot invites everyone to read a part of the Haggadah. I am happy he is being inclusive. One recurring phrase from the text derails my focus from the rest. Over and over we are told that God took the Children of Israel out of Egypt *with a strong hand and an outstretched arm.*

The first time we went on a date, Elliot walked to the driver's seat of my VW bug and stretched his arm over the car, his meaty cupped hand facing heaven. I loved this gesture. Later, putting his strong hand on my head during

Bonnie and Clyde cinched my decision. Of course I would marry him. I needed someone to take control, because I was twenty-four and afraid I might sleep with lots of Israeli men for the rest of my life and never have children, a family, Friday night dinners with candles, kiddush, challah, the works. This man was perfect for me: handsome like an idealized 1950s kibbutznik, emotionally withdrawn and controlling with a strong hand and an outstretched arm. We shared the same immigrant status and spoke English. He could save me from myself, or so I thought when we met in 1968.

* * *

Now it's time for dinner. I serve the gefilte fish, knaidlach soup, roast chicken, tzimmes, green beans, and salad. Before dessert we whiz through the second part of the Haggadah. Our goal is to get to the songs before everyone's too tired to sing. After "Next Year in Jerusalem," I serve an almond cake made with twelve egg whites. Then I suggest a change. "Let's sing 'Chad Gadya' first." This is the last song in the Haggadah, a playful Aramaic song about sequential killing. Israeli singer Chava Alberstein has turned the song into a political protest with dark insistent beats. I especially like her last verse:

> I changed myself this year.
> Once I was a lamb and a quiet kid.
> Today I am an insatiable wolf.
> I have been a dove and a gazelle.

Today I don't know who I am.

Elliot's eyes suddenly fill with yellow wrath because I have suggested a change. *He* is in charge of the seder. How dare I interfere and make a request. *Who are you?* he glares. *A disobedient dog? A naughty two-year-old?* "Who asked you?" he says.

The table quivers with embarrassed silence.

By now, in the late 1990s, I have become familiar with several sayings from the Talmud that deal with *malbin panim*, a concept that literally means making a person turn white. These aphorisms address the issue of insulting or belittling a person in public. One is "He who insults or belittles a man in public, it is as if he has shed that person's blood." Since shedding blood is a euphemism for killing, insulting a man in public is placed on the same level as murder.

Another saying goes "Better a man throw himself into a blazing furnace than insult a friend in public."

After my husband's attack, I feel small, ashamed, and guilty. These are familiar feelings and this is not the first time he has attacked me in public. But something on this night *is* different from all other nights. As I survey the stunned faces of my friends and family around the table, it dawns on me: I do not have to stay in this position. And then I tell myself: This is the last time.

I can leave Egypt. I *will* leave Egypt.

* * *

In "Pine," the story that unwinds in my head, after I stand with my back against the tree, my husband whips out his black pistol—Beretta? Colt?—from his belt over his right hip. He points it at me; I hold my breath. "Please don't shoot," I plead.

He shoots—click—aiming at my head. Nothing comes out but a limp plastic sound. He shoots again—click—aiming at my chest. He continues shooting, aiming at my waist—click—my pelvis—click—knees and feet. Click. Click. Click.

When he finishes playing this game, he puts the gun back into his pants, turns around, and strolls to the car. I exhale a sigh of relief: marital terror is not always lethal. I walk away from the pine and slide into the passenger seat. As we drive home in silence, I know I must unfasten my grip on inane hope, as well as its mate—fear of separation.

Tonight, when Elliot insults me in front of our family and friends, I do not throw Elijah's full cup of wine in his face or turn the table over with two outstretched arms. I do not shout at him to leave the house now, to get out of my life now, to leave me alone now, to leave, leave, leave. I am not a demonstrative woman and I avoid making scenes, other than those with tourists playing the roles of Rachel and Jacob at the cistern. Rather, I allow my emotional pain to simmer inside. I ache in silence, kneading the pain, analyzing it and intellectualizing it until the kneading, analysis, and intellectualizing make me crazy and helpless. Then, I cry on my pillow, dry my tears, and write a poem.

Tonight, however, I do not writhe in emotional pain. My self-esteem is not shattered. The part of me that for so many years needed to feel abused, abandoned, and emotionally ignored, as I had been as a child, that part, which I once thought was all of me but was not, that part, which was still a slave to longing for some romantic unconditional motherly love, withered. After twenty-six years of marriage, I have a new voice and I am not afraid of my husband.

Elliot can continue shooting words and glances at me like bullets, but he can no longer paralyze me from acting. Like the Children of Israel, I am free to leave. I am no longer a slave to tears and an outdated self-image.

Tonight, I see options. I can leave pining. I can take myself out of this cruel, debilitating, belittling game forever. My choice is to let go or suffocate, leave or die. This is my marriage's *hineni* moment—Behold! I am here. Behold! Here I am. And soon I will be out of here.

All this I realize as our guests sing "Adir Hu."

> God of Might, God of Right,
> who will build His house soon
> and quickly, soon,
> and in our own day.

During the interim days of Passover I announce to Elliot that I want to live separately for a few months. He protests. He refuses to leave, so I will take the step. He thinks I am still locked into our silent sick pact of not abandoning each other, but I have let go emotionally. He calls me at work and makes promises, but I have made up my mind. I recall the woman I met in the corner grocery store whom I hadn't seen in years. She was sixty-five and looked younger and more chipper than ever. When I asked her what had happened that made her so happy and youthful—Diet? Exercise? Love?—she said, "I left my husband."

After Passover I feel an enormous weight lifting from my back and shoulders. In June I find a three-room rental apartment across the street. It will be available on August 1. I am not leaving my children, I tell myself, in order to act. I am just moving across the street. There I hope to find *sheket nafshi*, peace of mind. After twenty-six years of living on a roller coaster, I am emotionally spent. The rental apartment is large enough so that the children can live with me, if they want. They are over sixteen and legally can decide for themselves.

I tell my husband this is not a divorce. "The family will still meet at the family home for Friday night dinners," I announce, insistent, fearful, and deluded.

On August 1, I move into the apartment across the street, taking only my clothes and a brown-and-white paper cut my mother gave Elliot and me for our first anniversary. In the paper cut a man holds up the words of Psalm 137. The words cover the perimeter of the art piece: "If I forget you, O Jerusalem, let my right hand wither. Let my tongue cleave to the roof of my mouth if I do not remember you, if I do not set Jerusalem above my highest joy."

From my rental apartment across the street from my family home, reading these words as I lie alone on my white Simmons Hide-A-Bed, I think about punishment. Judaism is full of commands to remember: remember the Sabbath, remember the Exodus, remember the mitzvoth, Zion, God. All this remembering, or else! I want to forget and start creating new memories. I do not deserve to have either hand wither or my tongue cleave to the roof of my mouth even for ten seconds. I have remembered enough.

Confusion and guilt are my punishments now, and they prevent me from finding the peace of mind I seek. My losses cry out to me from across the street: ema, mommy, mom.

A mother has left her children.

How can a mother leave her children?

I think of my own mother—not the woman who drove me to the orthodontist, summer camps, and college, not the mother who bought me *The Book of a Thousand Beautiful Things*, not the mother who sent me a postcard of *Boys in a Pasture* by Winslow Homer and wrote on the back "I know you'll feel at home with these fellas. Love &

Kisses." Rather, I think of the mother from 1951 who couldn't respond to my pain, the mother who was there and not there, unable to look into my eyes. I know I must accept and mourn this inner mother before I can give my children the love and attention they need and deserve.

Yes, it's my devastation with this mother of mid-twentieth century that has driven me to remain obsessed with Joey's death for so many years. I needed to stay obsessed until I had the courage to go back to the moment at the kitchen sink, to the woman standing in front of that sink, when the great and simple image of my mother, standing still, first struck root and in whose presence my heart not only opened but at the same moment also broke and closed.

Now I was sure my leaving Elliot was not tied up with my grieving for Joey. In the past I had been confused why I was so unhappy. Now it was clear to me. I could not grow in an abusive unnurturing environment. My self-confidence had grown. I was fifty-three. Time was running out. I was sure I did not want to spend it imprisoned.

A month before the seder, while I was building bricks, fifteen hundred retired Israeli army and police officers petitioned Prime Minister Netanyahu to stop settlement activity in the West Bank for the sake of peace. That's what I wanted—peace, quiet, separation. My country could not achieve that, but I could at least try.

Chapter Four: Saying No

Mourning becomes me. I am good at it, but now, a year after I left home, mourning does not dominate my life. I have dreams. One is earning an MFA in a low-residency program at Goucher College in Maryland. My mother is happy for me when I get accepted and invites me to visit her in Sarasota before the program begins. A widow, my mother lives by herself in a large home she and my father bought the year before he died. He was ninety-one and she was seventy-four. Her boyfriend, Gordon, whom she met a year after my father's death, lives in his own house. He and my mother make a snazzy couple, both athletic, he with a full head of white hair and she with naturally frosted short-cropped hair and a wrinkle-free face. Walking on the white sands of Siesta Key at sunset, they could be the stars of an ad sponsored by the State of Florida for the good life in the Sunshine State.

The white front door to my mother's coral stucco house is recessed, protected from sun and rain. In the alcove enormous crotons and ferns thrive. They are being well cared for by my mother. I am jealous. Everything spells lushness, even the floor mat that says "Welcome" and the ceramic planters that invite touch. Through the small window in the front door I see the broad living room, the screened-in porch with its turquoise swimming pool, and a man beyond in Bermuda shorts, standing on the fourteenth fairway of Palm Aire Golf Course, aiming at his hot-pink golf ball. Behind the pines of the golf course unwinds a skein of cumulus clouds.

I ring the doorbell and hear its surprising phrase, a perfect rendering of the first twelve notes of "An American in Paris." My mother probably spent hours choosing it. She, flawlessly coiffed, walks from the kitchen, drying her hands on a kitchen towel from Provence that is covered in sunflowers. She is robed in a stunning gray-and-turquoise caftan and adorned with delicate pearl earrings and an opal necklace, even though it is noon and she is doing the breakfast dishes.

"Why is your hair in your eyes?" she says, after "Hello." She moves aside so I can roll in my suitcase.

In the entrance hall, a French provincial table on top of which sit an antique doll, a coral quartz ashtray filled with keys, and a 1920s gold gaslight lamp make me feel I've fallen from some outpost on the moon into a photo op from *House Beautiful*. My mother straightens the hair on the antique doll and looks longingly at me. I am grungy, dirty, tired, and probably more full of germs than usual, after a long international flight. My four-year-old sandals, fake-leather purse unraveling at the seams, and cheap suitcase with orange yarn twisted around the handles for easy identification scream at me that they want to go home, home to the city on the hill where only the light is golden. I don't look like a refugee exactly, but neither do I look like I fit in this scene.

I push my suitcase into the guest bedroom, where twin beds are covered with quilted bedspreads with a baroque pattern. The busy yellow-and-navy-blue curlicues and fleurs-de-lis make me dizzy. A miniature quilted blanket with the same dizzying blue-and-yellow pattern covers the thick pillows on each bed, and a skirt around each bed with the same baroque design completes the picture. These are high-class frills. These beds are so well hidden it seems a shame to uncover them for sleeping. This is what I grew up with in Shaker Heights. I should be used to this norm, but after years in Jerusalem it seems ridiculously extravagant, the opposite of simplicity and necessity, values I have adopted in the Middle East.

This may be a difficult visit, I think, glancing at the valences over the two windows, covered with the same navy-and-yellow pattern. There are curtains hanging from the valence, as well as blinds, and even shutters and screens covering the windows, everything outfitted, shaded, and screened, layers and layers of stuff. All that is missing are angels on the ceiling, singing, "A, You're Adorable."

In the adjoining guest bathroom, miniature perfume bottles sit on a circular mirror placed in the corner of the marble counter. I recognize the names from the duty-free shop: Dior, Chanel, and Givenchy. Walking into the living room, I shrink before the white walls that soar twenty feet to the white ceiling. Above the four-seater pastel-peach couch, stuffed, pillowed, and inviting, hangs my mother's giant and favorite O'Sickey oil with its beautiful stillness: a romantic patio with two chairs and a table, draped in oranges and beige. Vivacious blues, greens, yellows, and magentas dapple the canvas in a celebration of garden and light. This is no Iowa farm scene on the verge of a tornado. That was my father's choice. But like the Iowa watercolor above my childhood couch, in this painting too, nobody stirs. The garden is empty, as are the exquisite peach-and-blue armchairs and white leather recliner in my mother's living room. In a room that beckons—come, relax, lounge—all I see, feel, and hear is *emptiness*.

Exhausted, I take off my sandals, plop down on the couch, and curl up in the corner, my bare feet touching a pillow with more fleurs-de-lis, these in turquoise and coral. I finger my way through *Better Homes and Gardens*, one of several magazines piled neatly on the coffee table under the lamp.

Does my mother think she's a queen? My father often treated her as one. Why do I feel more like the lady-in-waiting than the princess daughter?

As soon as I get up to walk into the kitchen for a glass of water, my mother appears behind me from her bedroom. As I turn to greet her she lifts the pillow my feet touched, shakes it out, pushes and slaps the couch back into shape, wipes it with a swift movement of her hand to rid it, no doubt, of particles of dirt from the Judean desert and traces of infection picked up from Continental Airlines.

She looks longingly at her couch and asks me if I want to look at photos. She takes out old albums before she even asks about the current crop of grandchildren. I have lost all agency that getting here demanded and revert to my passive, pliant, and pliable fourteen-year-old self. I will do whatever she says. We sit at the round marble kitchen table, speckled in pink, coral, and black. It is a beautiful table, but now it is covered with a cotton cloth of soft pink-and-green grapevines, the cloth lined with another layer of thick cotton. Curtains have curtains, pillows have pillows, and linings have linings in my mother's house, everything veiled and defended with impeccable protective coverings.

In one photo, from 1979, my mother and late father are surrounded by their three children and their spouses. Six beautiful, healthy grandchildren, all well-groomed, smile at the professional photographer. After spending some time looking closely and silently at this photo, my mother makes one comment: "I remember that table."

Indeed, standing perfectly stable behind the struggling young families, two of which will break up within twenty years, is a French provincial, leather-topped card table covered with a pansied tablecloth.

We continue to comb through family photos. My mother comes across one of herself and my father in 1968, celebrating my father's sixty-fifth birthday. In the photo she is forty-seven. Today she is seventy-nine. In the photo they are surrounded by cheerful, well-off friends, none of whom has yet succumbed to Parkinson's, arthritis, or Alzheimer's.

"Yes," my mother says with excitement. "That wallpaper! I remember choosing it for the new house."

She stands up to prepare us "something light for lunch" and I remain at the kitchen table, waiting to be fed. My insides constrict, shut down, and go to sleep. I know I will never please my mother. She will never take as much pride in me as she does in this table, that table, or the wallpaper. This is not an unfamiliar feeling, but if before there was doubt and disbelief that such a thing could be, now there is certainty, and more important, a new twin feeling: my mother will never please me.

Her setting, this scene is my mother's cover-up, this house more an elegantly shrouded fortress than a home. This place is a bunker, but who or what is the enemy? Maybe the onslaught of grief and loss. It's a trench for protection from sorrow, a stronghold that helps my mother hold herself together as she wards off memories of electroshock therapy, depression, and death. This is her comfortable dugout adorned with royal fabrics from which she can watch the playing field but never get dirty. From here, with her clean towels and sharp tools ("Look at my new knives!"), she can repel, drive back, fend off, rout the enemy, thinking all the while that it skulks without.

The invitation to relax and lounge in this sanctuary of luxury is an illusion, as empty as the warm painting above the couch. This Sarasota house is the Snow Queen's palace, and like her body, the house is unavailable for comfort, giggles, or tears. The Snow Queen is preoccupied with its brocade-rimmed lampshades, Limoges figurines, Waterford crystal, antique menorah, and French provincial credenza. There is no movement here. Beyond the eight-foot-high sliding doors, the turquoise water in the screened-in swimming pool barely ripples. Formal setting is all. Here, there is only setting, as there has always been. Stories get buried beneath layers of cushions, rugs, and heavy upholstery. Conversations don't happen. Here, one is frozen by the motionlessness of luxury, the stagnant eternity of beautiful things, the perfection of a garden hung on the wall.

Background is foreground for my mother. Wall coverings serve as important defensive ploys. Wallpaper can never desert you. A French provincial table can be restored to its 1950s sheen in a way that a toxic pregnancy can never be fixed. A couch cannot die and leave you when you are eight years old, like my mother's father did, leaving her bereft for the first time. Curtains will never suffer congenital spastic paralysis. A chair cannot die of pneumonia. It's safe to love furnishings, both hard and soft. With practice you become a woman of impeccable taste.

My mother's good taste, her insistence on proper appearances, and her love of interior design seem to be harmless solutions for dealing with loss. They hurt nobody except those closest to her, but close is a relative term when you're competing with wallpaper and tables, curtains and chairs.

When my mother looks longingly at her beautiful things I begin to understand that my crying, questing, and fantasizing about my dead baby brother Joey were emotional acrobatics I had to perform over the years in order to break out of my mother's static mode, to grow up and out of the frigid warm garden, to separate myself from her unexpressed pain. I begin to accept my delayed prolonged grief for Joey as my ticket to the interior design of passion. As a result, I am neither a figurine nor a chair, and most certainly not a wall.

Joey was my first encounter with death; my mother was my second. But whereas Joey never returned to the room with the white wallpaper and red farm animals, my mother was always there . . . and not there. Hers was an ambiguous death.

Perhaps this perplexing duality of being physically there but emotionally absent is one reason it has taken me so many years to come to terms with who I am.

"Thanks, Mom," I say when she places a plate with salad and bread in front of me. During the time in which she has prepared our lunch, I have traveled a journey that cannot be drawn by a narrow red line on a map of the world. I have come to an understanding about myself and my mother. I can read her now. I see who she is. When she sits at the table opposite me, I am overwhelmed with compassion.

During my one-week visit, in addition to going to the art museum, shopping for a new soap dish for her bathroom, and swimming in her pool, I accompany her to her volunteer work at the Anchin Pavilion for Memory Care. She is a new volunteer in the assisted living facility of the Sarasota-Manatee Jewish Housing Council.

On the second floor, around a table with six elderly people, my mother reads aloud newspaper headlines and sometimes full articles. The people around the table suffer from different levels of dementia. They listen and don't ask questions, but when they do, they ask the same question over and over again. My mother is patient. I am proud she still volunteers in her community and also curious about her choice.

"I have a big house, Judy," she says on my last day in Sarasota. "There's room for you here. Come home." She is standing at the kitchen sink, scrubbing a clean plate cleaner before putting it in the dishwasher. Her spotless chartreuse terrycloth shift ends just above the knees, revealing the tanned, muscular legs of a golfer.

"Home is a complicated concept," I say, placing four salad dressings in their appointed places in the fridge door.

"You've had enough of Zion," she adds as she scrubs another clean plate. She cleans as though she is trying to erase some defect that only she can see, as though her fashioned, correct, and orchestrated world would be perfect if she were able to erase that damn spot.

This is the first time in thirty-two years of Middle Eastern violence that my mother has told me to come back. Have I been waiting for this? Part of me once wanted my mother to tell me to leave Israel and come home. I thought that would mean she loved me.

That was many years ago.

And maybe I wanted her to ask me so that I could say no.

Since shedding my grief over Joey, I've been getting in touch with a feeling I once had: loving my mother. I remember strong, passionate feelings toward her when I was five, eight, and fourteen. Once I even tried to express the feeling. I was fourteen. My mother and I were standing in the kitchen of our new house on Lyman Boulevard in Shaker Heights. My parents had bought the house while it was being built so my mother could choose all the wallpaper, flooring, cabinets, and colors. She decorated the living room in French provincial and the family room in Early American, throwing herself into the task with fervor. The only time I ever saw my mother cry (after she cried about her lost hat) was the day she noticed that the turquoise tiles in the master bathroom were one shade darker than those she had ordered. She cried real tears for that lost shade. Nonetheless, she knew that the new house held sunny potential for happiness. It was on a corner lot, with an attached garage, and boasted a basement with a built-in shuffleboard, a Ping-Pong table, and a rec room with a record player and couch—a house, or at least a basement, clearly designed for fun.

On that afternoon in our new house, when I was fourteen, I walked up to my mother as she stood in front of the yellow fridge. "Can I give you a hug?" I said, both of us surprised, for I had never said such a thing before and we never hugged. Who expected such daring?

She put the dishtowel she held in her hand—Paul Revere riding to warn the troops—onto the pristine orange Formica counter. "Well. Let's see now. Yes. I mean, all right. I guess so."

Her words were enough. Maybe I suffered from body odor or my breath stank. Nonetheless, I put my arms around her upper arms and gave a stiff hug while she stood there, frozen. Afterward she found a pot to dry.

Years later I would understand that I wanted not only to hug but to be hugged by my mother.

Sometime after this cold hug, I began to wonder if my impulse for intimacy—for love—was dangerous. Would it only bring sorrow on me and possibly death for the one I loved? A confused teenager, I wandered from boyfriend to boyfriend in a never-ending state of unrequited love, unaware that beyond the tears of unrequited love hovered a strong longing for my mother. I was afraid of loving too much, because I thought my love may have the power to kill the beloved, not an unusual idea for a four- or five-year-old.

So strong is the memory of my love for my mother that now, standing in her Sarasota kitchen watching her scrub a clean plate cleaner, I seriously consider abandoning my full life in Jerusalem and moving to Sarasota. I want to come home. I want to have my mother all to myself.

I wonder if beyond the pull and call of a holy land, its hills that embrace, contain, and bestow meaning, is the sublimated longing for the mother's body.

My mother finally places one clean plate in the dishwasher and picks up another. I walk over to the marble kitchen table to straighten the tablecloth. I move into the living room and begin to arrange her pillows on the sofa. I appreciate how important my mother's soft static garden is for her stability. These fabrics and furnishings are her chosen children. They are the stable, loved objects she touches and adores. They surrender to her touch. These are the children that will never leave home.

The thick white carpet, the white walls, the French provincial chairs and credenza that she has treasured for fifty years, the elegant green-and-turquoise curtains that echo the rich upholstery, the sparkling clean glass doors that open onto her swimming pool—this is my mother's Eden.

I return to the kitchen, where she is still standing at the sink. She will always be standing at the kitchen sink. It offers support and security. A kitchen sink of Corian gray cannot die from rheumatic fever, like her father, from congenital spastic paralysis, like Joey. I stand next to her, shoulder to shoulder. Her scrubbing slows down to meaningless circular arm motions.

"I want to give you a hug, Mom," I say, standing next to her in the kitchen.

She puts down the plate and scrub brush, dries her hands on the exquisite towel from Provence, and turns toward me. I put my arms around her and rest my head on her right shoulder. After our breathing slows down, she leans into me, resting her head on my right shoulder.

"I love you, Mom." My voice is a whisper.

Her hands begin to rub my upper back in small circles. Slowly, the circles widen. It feels like every motion is pulling me closer to her, so that when the words start coming out of her mouth, slowly and softly, because they are diluted with tears, we are, finally, after years of emotional silence, one.

* * *

"I see the violence on CNN," my mother tells me on the phone from Sarasota. Outside my kitchen window in Jerusalem, combat helicopters of the Israeli Air Force fly over the block to attack the Al Aida refugee camp down the road. "Florida is calm," she says. "Come back."

She's probably sitting on the white leather chair in her living room, looking through the double glass doors at the pool and the golf course beyond. Jerusalem, on this night in January 2001, is violent and cold. Rotors chop light from the moon, and the pieces fall on my kitchen floor. Israel is retaliating for the Palestinians' gun fire into Israeli apartments in Jerusalem's Gilo, a contested neighborhood.

As the noise outside gets louder, my mother tells me to turn down the TV. "I have a big house," she says, "enough for all of you. Which army is your youngest in?"

My stomach muscles clench while the helicopters roar.

"Of course. Israel," she says, sounding ashamed of her lapse in memory. "Give yourself a rest, Judy. Lots of people are happy in Florida."

Ever since my visit two years ago, she has been loving and supportive in our phone conversations. "You teach intermediate conversational English to clerks at the Bank of Israel? Isn't that fabulous! And at Amdocs too? Wonderful!" Only a person with dementia can find something positive to say during an intifada that has injected fear into the entire population and halted tourism and thus caused me to lose my job at Neot Kedumim. I call her daily, not because of the local violence but because of her hospitalization at Sarasota General for the removal of an intestinal blockage. "Something is happening over there and it has to do with my meat," she said during the first postsurgery call. "I have a real nice waitress here."

In unblocking her gut, the doctors seemed to have opened the dam for dementia to flood everything.

* * *

Four months ago a Dr. Kaplan sat on the white leather chair in my mom's living room and asked her what day of the week it was. "Who is the president of the United States? When is your birthday?" After four hours he concluded that my mother suffers from "dementia of the Alzheimer's type."

My brother Jim, sister Elizabeth, and I thought he was mistaken. How could a beautiful woman with exquisite taste, an exemplary hostess who excels in small talk, a member of the John and Mable Ringling Museum of Art and Van Wezel Performing Arts Hall, a snazzy woman of eighty-one who drives a metallic-gray Honda Civic and cavorts with her beau, Gordon, how could such a woman be suffering from Alzheimer's?

We are an orchestrated trio called Sibs in Denial.

* * *

"I could use your help here, too," she continues, and then it registers: She needs someone to take care of her. She is asking me to come back, yet again.

Yet again my inner five-year-old is flattered and tempted. Little Judy could have her mother all to herself. Finally, Little Judy could hug her mother and her mother could read her the same book every night. Little Judy could drive her mother to psychiatrists. She could hold onto her apron for life. Judy could read her mother the same newspaper every day.

Behind every sentence I wrote about Joey hovered a longing for my mother. Joey was the umbilical cord to my mother. Now, when she deteriorates through Alzheimer's disease, my mother offers me an "opportunity" to experience that 1951 emotional pain once again, the pain of having my mother disappear. A mother there but not there.

"I'm afraid not, Mom," I tell her. Again. "I can't give up my new life in Jerusalem."

Today, being a mother trumps being a daughter. I want to stay near my three children in Israel. David, the man who rented my writing room, has become more than a friend. He is my anchor while I rebuild bridges and practice loving. Even though suicide bombers are exploding on buses, on sidewalks, and in coffee shops, even though a minor war is raging outside my kitchen window on this cold January night, I do not want to leave. Only now do I understand that loving is a mode of being, a stance like criticizing, judging, or ignoring, but healthier. On a daily basis I am choosing life and love. "I can't, Mom," I say, this time with sorrow. But I will not allow guilt to derail the life I am creating.

* * *

In a few months, Elizabeth, Jim, and I will accept that my mother cannot drive her car around Sarasota anymore and can no longer live by herself in her large house, even with Sherry, her caregiver who visits three times a week to cook and shop. We will help our mother move into a two-room suite at Kobernick House, the independent-living facility developed by the Sarasota-Manatee Jewish Housing Council. Sherry will visit her during the day to oversee her medications, take her to doctor's appointments, and make sure she doesn't put aluminum pans in the microwave to defrost hamburgers. Sherry will be the one who will eventually suggest we get rid of the microwave altogether. She will help our mother fake independent living and enable us sibs to continue our denial, despite our mother watering silk orchids every day.

None of us, however, will be able to deny our mother's diagnosis or hide it from the Kobernick staff, when, one night in 2004 at 3:00 a.m., a security guard will find her roaming the silent empty halls dressed in her impeccable pink nightgown, opening closets, and asking the walls, "Where is my lost child?"

Within two months we will move her to the Reinberger closed dementia ward at Judson Park in Cleveland Heights, five blocks from where she grew up.

* * *

My mother is still holding on at the other end of the line. The helicopters whirl back and forth in the dangerous darkness of night. A mad rain falls upon Jerusalem, and in this surreal setting I understand the root of the Joey obsession. He was not the only one who died when I was five. Yes, he was the first and he disappeared, solid gone.

My mother the second, but hers was an ambiguous death. There was a third death, as well. Part of me died too in that kitchen.

As the helicopters rumble, I mourn the little girl who grew into motherhood, one foot trapped in the past, glued in time and place under the linoleum floor, the Little Lost Judy, who is finally coming home to herself.

* * *

Maybe my father had been right. Maybe my mother *was* fragile and therefore he always had to protect her from the needs of her children. Perhaps, after the initial breakdown, he was afraid she would have a relapse and become a chronic psychiatric patient, in and out of clinics for shock treatments and who knows, maybe even mental hospitals, rather than becoming president of the Ludlow School PTA, president of the Women's Technion Association, and president of the Women's Association of the Cleveland College of Jewish Studies. Of course he would fear her becoming comatose instead of becoming a blue-ribbon flower arranger, a prize-winning golfer and bowler, a strong swimmer, dancer, and skater, an organizer, a volunteer, a woman who turned hosting and small talk into an art.

* * *

"I know, sweetheart," Mom says into her phone in Sarasota. "You have to take care of the kids. Just thought I'd ask."

"I love you, Mom," I say as our conversation comes to an end.

"Are you making lunch, sweetheart? . . . I love you, too."

* * *

Only when my mother will progress through the slow, tortuous deconstruction of a Self through the cruel paths of Alzheimer's disease will I be able to admit to myself that it was *I*, also, who preserved the distance between my mother and me after that day at the kitchen sink. I did not reach out for her, as Miriam reaches out for me, especially when I am reading in bed and she wants my attention. She demands that I listen to her. For this I am grateful and amazed. I dove underground, into an inner well. Lying on my back on the living room floor I watched television. Nursing my thumb, I sought substitute mothers. At four o'clock Kate Smith, with her big bosom, sang "God Bless America." At six Bob Smith made me feel part of something, even if it was called the Peanut Gallery. Fran from *Kookla, Fran and Ollie*, Beulah from *Beulah*, Molly from *The Goldbergs*, and Mrs. Hansen from *I Remember Mama*. But Miriam forces me to interact with her.

I became an agreeable, quiet, and exceptionally well-behaved child. When I dared to giggle, my father quickly put an end to it by staring at me as if I were an ant who had fallen out of line. I tried not to cause problems. My demands began and ended with "Please pass the syrup." I was the archetypal lost child, invisible to my mother and therefore myself and therefore, so I thought, to others. I became fiercely independent so as not to burden others, hiding in plain sight, even in my monogrammed sweaters.

In this condition of lost, I was anchored only by pencils, the dross of trees, slim sticks pushed left to right, and later right to left. What I recorded with those yellow pencils, on lined paper, in diaries, or cheap notebooks, were sounds from the well of sorrow—the longing, the mystery of some unattainable desire, some longed-for body I could touch and that would touch me.

* * *

After my mom and I say goodbye and hang up, her words—"Come back. I love you."—whiz around the cupboards like butterflies and land on the kitchen window, above the sink.

Chapter Five: Discovering

The friendly African American woman sitting at a window behind bars (Did people attack her for birth certificates?) reminds me of Lillian. I tell her my tale—that from my home in Jerusalem I requested a birth certificate for George Joseph Stonehill a few years ago and sent a payment that was refunded. "There's some legal glitch I don't understand," and as soon as I say "glitch" I wonder if that is English or Yiddish, but the woman with kind eyes does not falter or blink. "I'm in town for one more day," I explain. "Can you help me?"

She looks on her computer and turns to me with an apology. "I'm afraid it's going to take some time."

I don't want to spend any more time on Joey or my mother or 1951. I don't even want to be in Cleveland. The hall at the Office of Vital Statistics on Lakeside Avenue in downtown Cleveland is empty. I will lie down on the wooden bench and take a nap until Lillian returns with the birth certificate. "How long will it take?" I ask her. "I've already spent thirty years."

"Maybe ten minutes," she says and we both laugh. "I'll try to hurry."

I want to give her a hug, but the iron bars prevent all physical contact. The wooden bench accepts me until Lillian returns and motions me to her window. I wonder what will happen next. Did she find it? Will she give it to me? Was he born in Ohio? Do I need some legal document I don't have?

She asks for twenty-five dollars and I pay in cash. Under the lowest iron bar she slides me a white envelope the size of *The Family of Man*, a book that sat on our coffee table in Shaker Heights. I take the envelope and go sit on the bench, telling myself to breathe, thinking of Joey, the nineteen-month-old baby who died, not the monster obsession in my mind. I tear open the sealed envelope with care not to damage the gift inside. I pull out the document and stare. Light gray letters O H I O cover the darker gray background. This is my background too O H I O. I am proud to be a Buckeye, a Cleveland O H I O Indians' fan, a lover of Shaker Square O H I O and the celibate founders of the North Union Shaker Community in 1822 that became Shaker Heights Village O H I O in 1912, due to the capitalist and reclusive Van Sweringen brothers, O H I O railroad moguls who wanted to create a planned garden community in O H I O outside industrial Cleveland O H I O. Horseshoe Lake O H I O the grist mill O H I O the search for utopia in Northeast O H I O.

Slowly I steady my hand and my heart, fingering the document as if it were a fragment of a Dead Sea scroll, and I read.

It takes eight minutes, or six months and eight minutes, or six years and eight minutes, for the fact to register: Joey's name does not appear.

STATE OF OHIO
OFFICE OF VITAL STATISTICS

CERTIFICATION OF BIRTH

STATE FILE NUMBER	1949089926	DATE RECORD FILED	07/08/1949
NAME	STONEHILL		
DATE OF BIRTH	06/18/1949	SEX	Male
BIRTHPLACE	OHIO		
MOTHER'S NAME	RITA STONEHILL	FATHER'S NAME	NEAL STONEHILL
MAIDEN NAME	GROSSMAN		
MOTHER'S BIRTHPLACE	OHIO	FATHER'S BIRTHPLACE	IOWA

Note:

This is a true certification of the name and birth facts as recorded in the Office of Vital Statistics, Columbus, Ohio. Witness my signature and seal of the Department of Health this 11 day of June, 2014

State Registrar of Vital Statistics

CLEVELAND CITY HEALTH DIST

Chapter Six: Releasing

Raya practices shiatsu in a wooden house on a hill in Moshav Beit Zayit overlooking Ein Kerem. Wind chimes dangle outside the turquoise front door of her home. Water rushes over white Jordan River rocks in her electric-powered fountain next to the entrance. On their way to and from Africa, birds stop for a drink. Smells of rosemary and lavender, jasmine and geranium fill her living room, which serves as her clinic on this Monday morning. Dressed in loose cotton clothes, I lie on my back on the futon on the wooden floor in Raya's calm room. I want Raya to extract destroy shiatsu away my breathing tic.

Said tic, born in the kitchen on Ludlow Road in 1951, is often accompanied by a sharp pain in my upper back. In my imagination, this particular spot marks the place where my father's words entered my body. "Be quiet! Don't bother your mother!" After a lifetime of living with said tic and upper-back pain, I have noticed that it appears almost regularly whenever I drive away from someone I love. Of course, the loved one dies and I am distraught, even though said loved one is a healthy, functioning person. Clearly, my imagination is still too embedded in those magic years and believes my love can kill. After decades of various therapists who used words and wordy interpretations to help me grow, I am now ready to lie on a futon on a floor and have a therapist push her magic hands into that back place on my body.

High beige walls with big windows and large wooden beams on the ceiling offer a space both familiar and not. The beams remind me of the Western Reserve Historical Society Museum in Cleveland, where every fourth-grade school trip seemed to end. There, in a recreated one-room log cabin, mannequins of a pioneer family sat around a heavy wooden table, their faces lit by one (electric) oil lamp. In the quiet darkness of a pioneer evening a mother embroidered, a son carved a stick, and a daughter sat on the floor playing with a corn husk doll. A baby (doll) rocked in a cradle. The father—where was the father? My love for early Americana probably sprung from that idealized fatherless family.

Raya covers me with a lightweight quilt. She kneels next to my right hip and rubs her hands together to warm them before she touches me. She is a woman dressed in flimsy white cotton with a rich presence, and I am amazed I am actually here, allowing someone I don't know to touch and even massage my stomach. With her hands resting on my abdomen she asks where I'm from. I tell her Cleveland, though I would prefer not to talk. I want her to listen to my gurgling, swishing, and whatever sounds she hears through her fingers. She says she has a dear friend from Shaker Heights and stops the gentle touching. Shit. A therapist never did this. She proceeds to tell me about Shirley and Jack who used to summer in Beit Zayit and how S and J are like part of their family, and as we play Jewish geography, it turns out that this Shirley and Jack were good friends of my parents and that Jack, in the building supply business, helped my father package kitchen cabinets to send to his daughter Judy in Jerusalem in 1972.

Despite these golden nuggets of Jewish geography, I want Raya to shut up and work on my body, which she does, moving her hands over my liver and spleen, mapping the blockages in the meridians, determining the treatment for the next hour. I force myself to take a deep breath—I've learned what they are from yoga!—and tell myself this may not be nonsense.

Just as I settle down and get comfortable, Raya tells me to turn onto my stomach. She kneels by my head and places both her hands on my upper back. She leans in. I feel her weight and cough up phlegm. She says this may be phlegm that has been stuck in my body for many years. How many, I ask? She doesn't want to say, but I know the answer. This may be outrageous physiology, but it comforts me to believe that in 2005 I am coughing up waste that has stuck in my lungs, the seat of sorrow and grief, as every Chinese person knows, since 1951. My body teeters between East and West.

Raya rubs my shoulders, arms, hands, and fingers, both left and right. Then she leans into my back and moves her hands in circular motions. I sink into the futon and this surrender feels divine. "There, there," I say. "Press there."

"More," I say. "Press there."

"I feel it," she says.

"What do you feel?"

"It is like a hole, very deep. The more I press, the more it needs."

"More," I say, and then my stomach tightens and I contract it even more in an effort to curl inside myself like those rain jackets that fold into themselves and become small knots.

For the first time, someone in the real world is feeling the physical expression of my wound, the spot that mirrors the emotional hole in my soul, that homeland of familial grief, anger, longing, and love. My belief in this hole that has heft, the hole that is also a knot, is like the belief of the crazy historian with a theory about the size of Jerusalem in the eighth century BCE. Nobody accepts his wacko theory until one day an archaeologist finds a piece of the wall from the First Temple period that proves the historian was not crazy. Everyone apologizes to his widow.

"It's like an abyss," says Raya, this Israeli woman who grew up in a small moshav but visited Shaker Heights and is now traveling along the history of my back with her glorious hands. Raya rubs and kneads, pushes and pulls in an effort to loosen the knotty abyss from its surroundings, to bring it up to the surface, to pull it out and throw it away. She attacks from all angles and now goes for some of the meridians in my feet, legs, and head that will help her loosen the knotted hole, this paradoxical being of both entity and emptiness, there and not there.

A week later, while I'm lying on the same futon on my stomach, Raya is again kneading my back. I feel so relaxed

I cannot imagine ever getting up. After a few minutes she sees and I feel a sac or a bubble of liquid float out of my back.

"It's not a figment of your imagination," she says. "I felt it and saw it leave." This makes Raya the first person to confirm what I had always suspected: the hole in my soul has a parallel in the body.

* * *

Two months later I am on a plane to Cleveland, Ohio. When I enter my mother's room in Reinberger on this gray November day, my mother is in bed and does not recognize me—that is, she does not say, "Hello, Judy," but rather looks at me, kisses my face, and holds my hands in her wiry transparent hands. She is still alive and "in there somewhere" as her caretaker says. When she dozes, I sit in her white leather chair opposite her and stare at her face with seasoned concentration, searching for the woman from decades earlier, the mother I left when I went to climb Mount Zion.

She wakes up and I help her stand. We walk slowly, arm in arm, to the social area of the ward. It is time to sit in a circle with her demented friends and wave chiffon scarves to exercise the arm muscles. Awake, my mother only hums, so it is totally astounding when, at the end of today's visit as I kiss her balding head goodbye, trying to disengage in a graceful manner, she pulls me closer, as much as she can with her limp arms, and as I let go of her hand because I want to run into the elevator and out of this crazy place where sometimes I feel like I slide right in, she says two words, two comprehensible, sane words: "Come back."

Chapter Seven: Reenvisioning

It's safe inside the book. I want to stay here, with my fingers typing. Nobody can find me, inside the book. I'm hiding in my own story. Afraid to leave.

Sometimes we hear a voice and are called to go far away from our father, our kin, and our country. Once it was God. If we surrender to the call, we can reach a sanctuary with thousands of stairs, each stair a memory dream image word twitch inhibited breath. Each stair leads us back toward the sacred center. I believe in the center and I believe in the spine.

Perhaps the mountain of the Lord dwells within. Rather than climb, we dive into ourselves.

At the center of the center stands a mother at a kitchen sink. She wears an apron made by *her* mother. There I discover my first love for my mother, a love unsullied by thousands of small and large slights. This love-of-my-mother is the core proof of my ability to love. This ability is my greatest treasure. To love is a treasure. Not everyone can do it. So we should treasure this treasure. It is richer than the object of our love. Reconnecting with and enabling this treasure can save the lost child, the mourner, the whiner, obsessed, abused and abuser from loneliness.

Holding these thoughts and this love, I return to the tornado on Ludlow. I soften the memory with midrash, making it useful for today. My parents were good, decent people who cared for their children. They did not know how to express their love with nurturing words or physical closeness, locked, as they were, in their own shame, grief, and cultural moment. Finally, I can reenvision what happened.

I rewrite, therefore I am.

The Kitchen Sink

Snow is falling all over Cleveland and Shaker Heights, the Valley of God's Pleasure. Outside it is freezing, but in the living room at 2849 Ludlow, warmth prevails. Chocolate chip cookies bake in the oven, spreading their redolent fragrance throughout the house. Rabbi Green sits on the green living room couch, his face holding compassion and sadness like an offering, his hands holding ours, the hands of small children, lost and confused.

He gives us words: "Your brother died. Your baby brother Joey died. Now repeat after me. The Lord is my shepherd, I shall not want . . . Yea, though I walk through the valley of the shadow of death, I shall fear no evil, for Thou art with me . . . and I shall dwell in the house of the Lord forever."

He puts his warm hands on our heads and blesses us with calm words in a humble tone: "May the Lord bless you and keep you; may the Lord make his face to shine upon you. May the Lord be gracious unto you and give you peace."

His hands hold us in place as they bless and protect. We are not alone in our sad house. We are part of a tradition of grief and tears, poems and prayers.

I run into the kitchen crying, bawling, wailing, screaming, sniffling, and choking with sobs. My nose runs; tears blur my eyes. Fluids drown me inside and out. The kitchen is hot and full of smells. In addition to chocolate chip cookies in the oven, Grandma is making french toast and canadian bacon on the stove. Mommy is standing at the kitchen sink. Lilacs and daisies, purple and yellow, the colors of Ludlow School, cover the counter near the stainless steel sink. She is arranging a new world with flowers, one at a time. I grab the left side of her gray apron. Forsythia buds flutter over the apron like goldfinches coming home.

She puts down her scissors and wipes dry her damp hands. Then she bends her knees and kneels so her eyes meet mine. Green, gray, and white lines dance inside Mommy's eyes. They are beautiful, even more so through tears. Inside her navy slacks, her knees rest on the gray linoleum floor. Her arms are bare and she spreads them around me. I feel the tiny hairs on her arms and the blood moving in her veins and the warmth of her skin against my wet skin. Her arms hold me like the largest leaves in a flower arrangement encircle and protect the smallest bud.

"It is very sad, sweetheart," she says. "We all loved Joey, but he was very sick." I put my head against her chest and feel the words vibrate in her chest and in my ear. "We did the best we could." Then she holds me without saying a word. I sniffle and moan. She holds me. The longer she holds, the more my crying, sniffles, and moans subside and change to breathing. She breathes like me. We breathe together. If I hold my breath, I can hear the *ta-tum ta-tum* of her heart. That's how close we are to each other.

She lifts her right hand. I don't want her to get up, but she isn't getting up. With her right hand she touches my Buster Brown blond hair. Slowly and carefully she rubs my hair from the crown to the neck, as though she were patting a beloved cat. I purr, and somehow Joey's death hurts less. "He was a very special baby," Mommy says. "You were so good with him, Judy, the way you held him in the rocking chair, and so helpful to me, the way you stood next to me when I gave him a bath. I know you loved Joey, sweetheart. We are so sad that he could not show us his love."

I stop breathing because I want to catch every word, to hold on to each word like I hold on to the handlebars of my four-wheeler. For life. I am a big girl and getting bigger, but sometimes I fall. Next year I will start first grade. Now I want to carve these words inside. Where is that place? With my right pointer I twist the hair over Mommy's ears. She laughs and says, "That tickles." The smells cover me like a warm blanket. I don't know what I love more, the smells or the tastes or my mother's words.

Elizabeth walks into the kitchen and Mommy goes from kneeling to plopping her tush on the floor. She opens her legs wide so we can both sit inside her. She holds me with her left arm against her left side and Elizabeth with her right arm against her right side. I reach out for Elizabeth's hand and Lizzie doesn't say yuk, even though my hand is slimy from my runny nose and tears. "Daddy and I are very sad," Mommy says. "We cry every night. The rabbi says God will be good to us." Now she touches both our heads and gently moves the hair out of our eyes. "We hope he is right."

Daddy walks into the kitchen. "The rabbi just left," he says quietly when he sees Mommy, Lizzie, and me on the floor in front of the kitchen sink. Mommy turns and lifts her face to him and smiles with her mouth closed, her eyes closing, and I can feel something move inside near her heart. She is crying a silent cry. Daddy stands behind her, his legs supporting her back. His breaths cross the top of my head and tickle my ears. Now he bends down too and stretches his arms over all three of his girls. "We're like a mountain," he says and we all giggle.

"Like a flower arrangement," Lizzie says.

"Like a Stone Hill," I say, and we all shake from laughing, and now even Daddy has plopped onto the floor behind Mommy. Our laughter turns into tears. We heave like one body for the one body that didn't work right, the Joey body, who is no longer with us but only inside, Joey, who is here and not here. I marvel at how this plumbing system we all have inside turns our laughter and sadness into liquid and how this liquid flows from both eyes and these tears turn into words and then we feel spent, emptied, squeezed clean from inside.

Time stops. The sun breaks through the falling snow, and its rays shine through the kitchen window. It anoints us with light, all four of us piled on the kitchen floor, and Grandma too, standing by the stove, watching, listening, and cooking. If I stick out my tongue, the light will taste like maple syrup.

Daddy puts a hand on my head and it feels large and safe. He says, "Judy, Judy," as if he wants to save me, "Judy, Judy," this time as if he wants me to save him, and again he says, "Judy," as if we all need saving, and now he looks from one end of the kitchen to the other and says in his Jackie Gleason joking voice, "Judy, will you please bring your dear old dad one of those cookies your grandma and mom have been baking forever, wherever the hell they are," and Mommy turns her head to look at Daddy and even stretches her right arm to put her hand on his cheek and says, "Honey, you're so full of Iowa corn, it's growing out of your head."

Postscript

Weep not for the dead in excess, neither bemoan him beyond measure. How is that applied? Three days for weeping and seven for lamenting and thirty to refrain from cutting the hair and donning pressed clothes. Thereafter, the Holy One, Blessed Be He, says, "You are not more compassionate towards [the departed] than I."

Babylonian Talmud, Mo'ed Katan, 27b

Acknowledgments

Thank you to Elana Sztokman of **Lioness Press** for hearing my inner lioness and believing in my nontraditional memoir.

Parts of this book appeared in slightly different versions in the following publications: *Lilith Magazine* (2017); *Ilanot Review* (2017, online); biostories.com (2020); and *Evening Street Review* (2021). I am grateful to the editors of these publications.

Thank you to Terry Benninga, Joan Leegant, and Amital Stern for their encouragement and help along the way, and to Deborah Meghnagi Bailey for her initial editing. Thank you to members of the Best Book Club Ever for your support and friendship.

My writing students over the past twenty years at The Writing Gym, David Yellin College, The Writing Pad, and Rewriting Groups have taught me more than I taught them. Their questions made me a better writer, as the questions of my therapists over the past fifty years have made me a more conscious person.

Allen Hoffman, American-Jewish writer in Jerusalem, has always been encouraging, along with fiction and nonfiction mentors Mark Mirsky, Steve Stern, Lauren Slater, Lisa Knopp, Diana Hume George, Phil Gerard, and Fred Leebron. Thanks to Marcela Sulak and members of her inspiring Tel Aviv writers' salon.

My cousin George Becker and his mother, Aunt Nat, provided much-appreciated support during difficult days in Cleveland. I am grateful to my sister and brother for their cooperation.

My children deserve hours of quality time they missed when I was obsessed with their phantom uncle. My love for them and their families overshadows all guilt.

David Kurz has taught me patience and acceptance. His love and constancy enabled me to complete this project.

In Memoriam

Neal Stonehill, 1903–1992   Rita Faye Grossman Stonehill, 1920–2014

George Joseph "Joey" Stonehill, 1949–1951

Made in the USA
Coppell, TX
14 June 2023

18077403R00184